Great
Company
Crashes

Great
Company
Crashes

by A.F.L. Deeson MA PhD DSc

LONDON

W. Foulsham & Co Ltd

NEW YORK . TORONTO . CAPE TOWN . SYDNEY

W. FOULSHAM & CO. LTD.,
Yeovil Road, Slough, Bucks., England

ISBN 0 - 572 - 00833 - 3

© Copyright W. Foulsham & Co. Ltd. 1972

Made & Printed in Great Britain by
Bristol Typesetting Co. Ltd.
Barton Manor - St. Philips
Bristol

Contents

Death of a Newspaper

The Sunday Advertiser
1807-1829

THE *Sunday Advertiser* cannot claim to be a 'great' business collapse with far-reaching repercussions such as those which followed the City of Glasgow Bank failure, or, for that matter, the debacle of Fire, Auto and Marine.

Nevertheless it is of interest because it was one of the first Sunday papers to be published in England (the *British Gazette and Sunday Monitor*, which saw the light of day in 1780 was the pioneer of Sunday journalism), and its brief history is unusually well documented thanks to the efforts of an American research student, Basil L. Crapster, to whom I am indebted for much of the information contained in this chapter.

It is also worth bearing in mind that 'greatness' in collapses, as in other matters, is relative and, by and large, the dramatic and resounding failures that have been an increasingly common feature of the commercial and industrial scene during the last 50 years were, at the turn of the last century, almost completely unknown. Thus, although the story of the *Sunday Advertiser* is set in London it has a rural character and an easy pace absent from most of the other studies in this book.

Although a legitimate forefather of the modern mass-media

Sundays, the whole structure of the economics of the *Sunday Advertiser* was, as one might expect, completely different from that of its successors a century and a half later. Encouraged by the success of Mrs Elizabeth Johnson's *British Gazette and Sunday Monitor* there had been a proliferation of Sunday newspapers around the beginning of the 19th century and by 1813 London had 14 Sunday papers—but together they had a circulation of only 26,000.

Although long since forgotten, the *Sunday Advertiser* itself had a connection with a very famous daily newspaper which is still in existence: the *Morning Advertiser*, the daily newspaper of the public house trade. The *Morning Advertiser* was founded as long ago as 1794 by a group of London publicans, the Friendly Society of Licensed Victuallers, and its successor, the Licensed Victuallers Association, is to this day a living force in pub politics.

When the *Morning Advertiser* was first published subscription to the paper was a prerequisite of membership of the Society and all profits were devoted to the Society's benefit fund. In 1803 the Society accepted a new responsibility when it opened a school and orphanage for members' children at Kennington. Demands for admission were heavy and the existing sources of revenue, principally grants from the Society's general fund and special subscription by members and friends, soon proved insufficient. So, following the success of the *Morning Advertiser*, the *Sunday Advertiser* seemed a promising venture to provide the school with the funds required.

At that time there were high hopes of a big market for Sunday newspapers because many people, either because of shortage of time or money, confined their newspaper reading to Sundays and in those days publicans made newspapers available on their premises to attract customers. During the week they had the *Morning Advertiser* and other newspapers but on Sunday, which was one of their busiest days, nothing which they could call particularly their own and which would put over to their customer news and views which they wished to promulgate. There were other attractive considerations:

because the *Morning Advertiser* was only published six days a week both staff and plant were idle on Saturday. Nor were high editorial expenses contemplated because most Sunday newspapers at the time were little more than rewrites of material from the dailies.

On 13 April 1807 30 licensed victuallers agreed to get the paper under way by subscribing £10 each—a grand total of £300. In addition the *Morning Advertiser* advanced £218 for advertising bills and other initial expenses. It was agreed that the new paper should use the *Morning Advertiser*'s publishing premises at 11-12 Catherine Street off the Strand and W. Perryman, the morning paper's printer was invited to undertake the printing and gladly assented. William Perryman, the printer, was quite famous in his own day and was twice prosecuted, once in 1788 for a libel on Pitt and the House of Commons in connection with the impeachment of Sir Elijah Impy and in the following year for a libel concerning the King's health. He also printed the *Morning Herald*, copies of which are still in the British Museum as, incidentally, are also a few copies of the *Sunday Advertiser*. It was agreed that the *Morning Advertiser* should pay all the expenses of printing and publishing but that the *Sunday Advertiser* should then reimburse its daily companion to the extent of one-sixth of the total expenses incurred.

The first issue of the *Sunday Advertiser* appeared on 17 May 1807 and 1,700 copies were sold at 6d each. This, for the time, was a very good start and better was to follow: weekly sales soon reached 2,000 and advertisement revenues from manufacturers and others wishing to reach not only the licensed trade but also their customers were excellent. In March 1808 £123 was given to the school by way of profit and it was generally felt that a good beginning had been made. By September of the same year it was agreed that the original 30 proprietors should be repaid and they were, including one who, as Basil Crapster has pointed out, never in fact paid his promised subscription in the first place. At the same time it was agreed that as each of the 30 died his place on the committee was to be filled by election by the Society's membership from among the trustees or management committee.

In spite of the early commercial successes of the *Sunday Advertiser* the few copies which have come down to us give little indication of journalistic talent, even allowing for the differing standards of the time. The editor seemed to have a prejudice against late news, possibly because he did not want to work on a Saturday afternoon and the majority of material was lifted straight from the dailies of the preceding week. While the *Sunday Advertiser* differed from other Sunday papers of its time in that it advertised licensed premises for sale and notices of meetings of various trade associations and charities, there was otherwise very little to distinguish it from any other Sunday. Usually it contained theatrical notes, City 'intelligence', letters to the editor, notices of bankruptcies, comments on Parliamentary proceedings, bits and pieces from the foreign papers, news of ships arriving and departing and accounts of crime and police court proceedings. Apart from the specialised advertising there were the usual advertisements of medicines and lotteries, and notices of births, deaths and marriages. Crimes and police court proceedings were popular and the *Sunday Advertiser*, trading on the experience on the *Morning Advertiser* in that direction, always gave them plenty of space. For example, enlarged editions of both papers appeared to report the outcome of the trial of the Cato Street conspirators in 1820.

Because of the non-original character of a great deal of the material it is not surprising to find that at one point the committee of management questioned whether the editor of both papers needed to subscribe to five other journals and use the services of two permanent reporters. In addition it was noted that extra reporters were taken on for Parliamentary reporting during the session. However, after a good deal of discussion the editor got away unscathed.

Generally the *Sunday Advertiser* was anti the Government in power (the Whigs) but never, on the other hand, outstandingly radical. It appears to have been aimed at an upper working class and lower middle class public; its leaders were always extremely righteous, as befitted a Sunday newspaper, and contrasted sharply with the enthusiasm which it displayed elsewhere for juicy stories. As such it was attacked from time to time for its sensationalism. A petition to the Prince Regent of 17 September 1812 includes the *Sunday Advertiser* in a list of Sunday papers described as dangerous because of their anti-ministerial, pro-French position and their appeal to lower class minds and pocket books. One doubts if Prinny was unduly disturbed.

The halcyon days of the *Sunday Advertiser*'s success were really very limited. In 1808 it had an average weekly circula- of 1,809 copies and during the year published 1,242 advertisements.

In 1809 the average weekly circulation had fallen somewhat to 1,710 copies but the advertisements had risen to 1,636.

There is a gap in the records for the years 1810-13 but in 1814 the circulation was down still further to 1,557 copies although advertising was still slightly up on the first year at 1,338 advertisements. From then the circulation fluctuated, never reaching the first year's record of 1,800. In 1822 it fell to 1,300 copies and by 1827 the average weekly circulation was only 972 although it made a strong rally in 1828 when it acquired an average weekly circulation of 1,485.

Much more to the point, however, was the continual decline in advertising. From 1816 until its final death it dipped every year until at last only 235 advertisements were published in 1828—an average of less than five a week. Unfortunately, the *Sunday Advertiser* got weaker as the Sunday press as a whole got stronger. When it started in business its circulation was a good average but the public's taste for Sunday newspapers caught on fast and by 1826 the *Observer*, then as now a leading paper, claimed a circulation of 10,000.

The Society seems to have ignored the gradual erosion of circulation and the decline in advertising revenue, and maintained an unfailingly optimistic approach to the whole venture. For the most part the *Sunday Advertiser* jogged along. In

1815, when stamp duties on newspapers were raised, the price was increased to 7d and in the same year both papers moved to premises on a newly purchased freehold at 127 Fleet Street on the corner of Shoe Lane. Then, in 1818 the paper was enlarged, a new type was introduced and a new printer appointed. The editor took this opportunity to make a policy statement which appeared in the paper on 4 January 1818:

'We shall carefully abstain from being garrulous and unnecessarily diffuse, being rather anxious to give the spirit and substance of all matters worthy of notice, always strictly adhering to facts, and never descending to impose on the Public by marvellous stories unfounded and untrue, merely for the purpose of forcing a temporary and precarious sale. With respect to the politics of the Paper, they are well known. THE SUNDAY ADVERTISER is devoted to the CAUSE OF THE PEOPLE, and the true interests of the Country. In supporting these it will be firm, yet temperate—diligent in the pursuit of morality and facts, we shall never suffer its columns to be polluted or disgraced by personal slander, or by anything that may be considered unworthy or reprehensible in a Public Print.'

Unfortunately all this effort only obtained a very small increase in circulation the following year and even this was accompanied by a further drop in advertisements.

By June 1821 the committee could no longer ignore the situation and while no figures have come down to us it seems that they must have been making small losses at this time. The printer, and editor were asked to cut costs and they were successful enough in this to report a profit of £32 for the quarter ending in September 1821. Meanwhile, on 12 August the 740th issue of the paper had appeared with slightly longer columns under the new title, the *Sunday Advertiser and Weekly Register*. The reasons for this change are unknown but on 12 January 1823 the title of 'Sunday Advertiser' was dropped altogether and the newspaper became the *Weekly Register*. While the paper continued to appear on Sundays it may be that the proprietors intended to compete with the weekly 'local' newspapers which were at that time just beginning to appear in London and hoped that the change of name might give the paper a longer currency: in other words, perhaps they hoped to sell it throughout the week and not just on Sundays. This may, in part, have been successful because profits were reported at £127 in 1822 and the following year, when steam printing was introduced and consequent economies reported, the profits rose to £194, of which £150 was put in a reserve fund. Apparently the orphan school was not getting much out of the venture.

In 1824 the fund was credited with £16 and £20 in 1825 but the following year was a bad one and wiped out the reserve. In 1827 there was a loss of £37. By then they had a new printer, J. Brown, and in spite of the precarious position of what was now the *Weekly Register* two Napier presses were ordered in October 1827 at a cost of £1,100, although no doubt the much better based *Morning Advertiser* paid the greater part of this cost. Enthusiastic plans were announced for a paper 'equal to any other, enlarged to four folio pages with 20 columns at the same price and supported by an expanded reporting establishment'.

At the same time there was going to be yet another new name. Apparently the proprietors had once more decided to go all out for a Sunday paper and it was to be known as the *Sunday Herald*. It was also agreed that the *Morning Advertiser* editor had enough on his plate already and advertisements were placed for a new and separate editor for the *Sunday Herald*. Applications were received from four candidates but on 27 November 1827 it was decided that both papers should continue to have the same editor. By then the editor of the *Morning Advertiser* had resigned so the need was urgent.

A. Franklin was offered the job of sub-editor on both papers at four guineas a week, an appointment which he accepted. Franklin was connected with the *Morning Advertiser* from 1818 to 1830 and perhaps longer. Crapster has suggested that he may be the Franklin who ran the *Morning Herald* for three years and then the *Morning Post* until 1796. Or he may have been the 'Franklin' mentioned as editor of the *Public Advertiser* in the 1820s, an Irishman who emigrated to England in 1777 at the age of 22. Crapster has also pointed out that the British Museum Catalogue lists an Andrew Franklin, a playwright, who died in 1848 and an Abraham Franklin who was an author of radical pamphlets on banking in the early 19th century.

When Franklin was appointed the committee decided to give the editor seven guineas a week. The applications for the position have remained on record and provide an interesting picture of the journalist as he was then. John Anderson, aged 32, who eventually got the job proffered his knowledge of French, Italian, Greek and German and presented testimonials from *The Times* and Joseph Hume, Member of Parliament. Crapster suggests he may be John Anderson of Aberdeen who graduated from the University there in 1813.

James Haynes, who was a close runner-up, was already a staff member of the *Morning Advertiser* and offered references from other journalists. The other applicants were S. G. Montagu Denton who claimed a knowledge of French, German and Italian together with six years journalistic experience, including the provision of Parliamentary and other intelligence to provincial newspapers through the County Newspaper Office; and W. H. Fitzpatrick of the Middle Temple who was also aged 32, offered no testimonials, but indicated a knowledge of Greek, Latin and French and long experience as editor of several papers. However, he subsequently withdrew his candidacy, perhaps because he had obtained another job in the meantime.

Although the committee had previously decided to give the editor seven guineas, in fact they went back again to the idea of providing the *Sunday Herald* with its own editor and thus Anderson was promised a salary of only five guineas a week but with a rise of £25 a year for each 250 increase in the weekly circulation. The last issue of the old paper announced the acquisition of the services of 'a gentleman, whose talents and experience have already proved of eminent service elsewhere, and from whose zealous co-operation we confidently anticipate the most decided success.'

Unfortunately the *Sunday Herald* was doomed from the very beginning. Although at the quarterly meeting in September 1828 both advertisements and circulation were 'considerably over' the equivalent quarter of the preceding years, in December the committee was again anxiously discussing the paper's future. They wondered if it should come out on a Saturday instead of Sunday because, in the absence of a Sunday post out of London, the country circulation was bound to be small. On the other hand, papers coming out on Saturday had no chance of covering the week-end news from Saturday onwards. Some papers tried to overcome this by producing a Saturday edition for country circulation and then a Sunday paper for the metropolis, but the Stamp Office had effectively squashed this piece of commercial initiative by decreeing that Sunday papers which brought out a Saturday edition for country circulation must pay a double advertisement tax, even if the two editions were identical except for the dateline.

Nevertheless, the Sunday newspaper boom was on and, almost weekly, competitors appeared, which may have had something to do with the circulation and revenue problems of the *Sunday Herald*. A contemporary journalist, Gibbons Merle, quoted by Crapster, pointed out in an article in the *Westminster Review* that Sunday newspapers were then a prime target for entrepreneurial activity and that speculators needed only £20 capital and a day's notice to be a newspaper proprietor.

In January 1829 the life of the *Sunday Herald* was fast drawing to a close. In the last quarter of 1829 sales averaged 1,557 weekly and there had been a loss for the year of £37. It was estimated that to make a profit—and this should have been estimated a long time ago—a weekly circulation of 3,000 to 4,000 was necessary, whereas the Society had only about 2,000 members in business and had always largely relied on them for circulation. A sub-committee got down to the problem with a thoroughness which its predecessors might have displayed. They showed that the profits claimed in some years were in fact not profits at all, that the Sunday paper, published for expressly this purpose, had made only two contributions to the school, £123 in 1808 and £159 in 1818; yet the paper had never repaid a farthing of the money advanced at its foundation by the *Morning Advertiser* and had not even paid its promised one-sixth of the overheads. It had benefited from, but had hardly helped to finance, the costly improvements in plant made by the *Morning Advertiser* and, the sub-committee suggested, it was in fact living on the capital of its daily stable companion and costing the latter something like £100 a year. Further, the committee asked that it should be fully noted that competition was growing. Already at the beginning of 1829 three new weeklies had been announced and rival papers published on Saturday to catch the night coaches to the country had eaten into sales. Finally it was noted that John Anderson, perhaps disillusioned, wanted to resign the editorship.

Perhaps, as Crapster has suggested, there was another fundamental weakness. Could a newspaper, even in the more leisured days of a century and a half ago be supervised by a committee of management? Certainly it could not today and Robert L. Haig, historian of *The Gazeteer*, which had its life from 1735 to 1797, has suggested that by 1797 control by a management committee had become obsolete, however efficient that committee might appear to be. Today no newspaper or magazine could possibly be run efficiently or effectively by either a management or an editorial committee and there are indications that the supervision was very close indeed, which may explain why journalistically the paper, under a number of editors, was always so undistinguished.

The committee that managed the *Sunday Advertiser* and its successors had the added disadvantage that they were dealing in a media which was totally unfamiliar to them as publicans. This, presumably, is the reason why the paper's financial condition was not formally recognised for so long, and yet the Society's other ventures were carefully administered. Perhaps they didn't like to admit failure or was it simply bad book-keeping? It is also fair to point out that the *Morning Advertiser*, which is still flourishing, was run by the same committee although at that time it was itself ailing and it wasn't until 1850 or even later that it really got onto its feet.

The sub-committee's recommendations were to raise circulation or to sell out and the latter course was recommended. With circulation high, as it always was in the winter months, an immediate sale was suggested and it turned out that a prospective purchaser was at hand. William J. Clement, the first of the newspaper barons, who then owned the *Morning Chronicle* and three weeklies, was looking for further expansion and was currently negotiating in several directions at attractive prices. He had offered the Society £1,000 for the paper in 1824 when circulation had been at about 1,100 and he now offered 700 guineas with the idea of merging it with another of his weeklies, *The Englishman*.

On 12 January 1829 the trustees of the Society, accepting the conclusions of their sub-committee, wrote to Clement suggesting he return to his previous offer of £1,000 cash. Clement countered with an offer of £800, a promise to subscribe to the *Morning Advertiser*, a 10 guinea life subscription to the school, and the promise to carry free marriage and death notices of the Society's members. Settlement was finally made at 800 guineas, a very good price one would have thought for those times and bearing in mind the history of the paper.

The last issue came out on 8 February 1829 and a week later transfer of the property took place. All formal connection with the Licensed Victuallers was severed.

For some unknown reason Clement did not merge his new acquisition with *The Englishman* but with another paper of his called *The News* and which then came out as the *News and Sunday Herald*.

In the end Clement over-reached himself, his empire con-

B

tracted and in 1834 he sold his beloved *Morning Chronicle*, reportedly at a loss of nearly £30,000.

By then, however, the failure of the *Sunday Advertiser* was only a bad memory to the Society and at any rate, unlike many of the other stories recorded in this book, the Society had harmed no one by their failure. Although it didn't get much help from the *Sunday Advertiser* (a final payment of £28 was made in 1829 in addition to the other two payments already mentioned), the Licensed Victuallers School exists to this day.

CHAPTER 2

Bankers in Trouble

The City of Glasgow Bank
1839-1878

THESE DAYS the integrity of the British banking system
is beyond question and failures are unheard of; but not
a hundred, or even 50 years ago.

Between 1850 and 1920 there was a regular succession of
closures, caused by unwise investment, bad management, or
downright fraud. Businessmen, farmers, retired people, widows
and children all suffered and were sometimes ruined—until,
tardily, the regulations concerning the management of a banking enterprise were tightened up and the many gaps were
effectively stopped.

Of the many failures that occurred in the last century,
possibly the largest and certainly the most dramatic, was that
of the City of Glasgow Bank which, it transpired, was partly
caused by careless investment but mostly by a series of frauds
by the directors of the bank.

The failure—to the tune of well over £6 million—was a
disaster for Scotland and, indeed, for the whole country. The
bank was the largest in Scotland with 133 branches and issued
its own notes. Hundreds of concerns and thousands of individuals were impoverished by its closure. It caused at least
three suicides and two mental breakdowns. A Scottish financial
expert said as recently as 1968 that the repercussions were

still apparent in some sectors of the Scottish economy 90 years afterwards.

Writing at the turn of the century William Wallace, that indefatigable commentator on public trials stated, in the round language of his time :

'The magnitude of the financial crisis brought about by the collapse of the Bank, the social standing of the Directors to whose hands the management of it was entrusted and who so shamefully abused the confidence reposed in them, the un-paralleled disclosures of financial turpitude and recklessness revealed in the report of the professional gentlemen who con-ducted the preliminary investigation of its affairs immediately after the stoppage, and the startling nature of the evidence adduced by the prosecution, all combined to invest the trial with an interest which is not surpassed in the annals of our criminal jurisprudence. That this financial disaster, which brought ruin to so many homes, depriving in many instances the widow and the orphan of their sole means of maintenance, was brought about, not by innocent misfortune, but by the criminal recklessness of men whose commercial probity, high social standing, and professed religious belief had induced thousands of their fellow-countrymen to place implicit trust in their honesty and integrity, only serves to intensify the interest felt in their trial. How these men abused the confidence re-posed in them—how, by insidious steps, they converted a once-sound and prosperous banking concern into a mere machine for the abstraction of the hard-won savings of the small and all-too-confiding investor, only to throw them into the lap of wealthy and unscrupulous speculators, who were thus enabled to dissipate them in schemes of reckless folly and insensate gambling—how, while posing as pillars of commercial inte-grity, they were in reality the rotten props of a decaying and worthless concern—may be seen from a perusal of the evidence adduced for the prosecution, of the brilliant and incisive speech of the Lord Advocate and of the no less luminous and weighty charge to the jury of the learned Lord Justice-Clark.'

The City of Glasgow Bank began business as a banking concern in 1839, first establishing its head office in Glasgow and soon opening numerous branches throughout Scotland. It continued to carry on business, more or less uneventfully, until the end of 1857 when a general financial crisis hit Britain and was particularly hardly felt in Scotland. At that time the Western Bank of Scotland closed its doors for ever and the City of Glasgow Bank also suspended payment.

However, a number of influential men in the City resuscitated it and it again resumed business in the beginning of the year 1858, paying out to all investors.

It was registered under the Joint Stock Companies Act of 1862 and continued its operations until it finally ceased to do business and its doors were closed for ever on 2 October 1878.

There were in all 1,249 'partners' or shareholders connected with it and at the time of its closure its paid up capital amounted to £1 million. At the beginning of 1878 the reserve fund was stated at £450,000, the dividends and surplus profits in hand at £148,501, the deposits at £8,382,712 and the 'circulation, acceptances etc' at £2,114,229. In December 1875 the price per £100 of stock had been quoted at £228; in 1876 £228 again and in 1877 £243.

To all intents and purposes the Bank was a prosperous business, but early in 1878 some of the more knowing sections of the financial community began to suspect that something might be amiss. However, it was not until September that concern started to spread through the City and investors in the country districts had no suspicion of trouble until the Bank actually closed its doors. In informed circles concern was expressed that the Bank had an unusually large number of acceptances floating in the London market and this gave rise to suspicions of some pressure. At the same time old comments that the directors were prepared to lend a little too freely to speculative ventures and to give credit at some risk, were revived. Nevertheless the stock kept up well until the end—it was £236 on the closing day—and the more confident or optimistic sections of the community pointed to the fact that as recently as August a 12% dividend had been declared.

But then, on Tuesday 1 October 1878 at a little before noon, the directors resolved to stop the Bank and within an hour their decision was all over the City, followed by another announcement that the managers of the other banks had met and had agreed that to lessen the inconvenience to the public they would receive and cash the notes of the City of Glasgow Bank then in circulation.

This latter news allayed an immediate panic. It was generally assumed that if the other banks were prepared to cash-in the City of Glasgow Bank's notes the situation could not be too serious and the depositors must be covered.

Nevertheless the more farseeing businessmen in the City were uneasy. The rapid recovery of the Bank from the 1857 crisis and the steady rise of the value of its stock and dividends had, apparently, attracted many small merchants and tradesmen, widows and retired people either to invest as shareholders or to entrust their savings as depositors. On close scrutiny the list of shareholders did not inspire much confidence among the businessmen in the City; it was largely made up of private individuals and it later transpired that a considerable number of those holding shares had had advances made to them by the Bank to the extent of their holdings. On 2 October large quantities of the stock were put on the market and the prices fell steeply, although there were few takers. The realisation of the possible extent of the calamity was only just dawning on the financial community and, as the implications became more and more obvious, the shares dived steeply.

On the same day the directors placed the books of the Bank in the hands of a firm of accountants and a firm of solicitors with instructions to investigate and prepare a report of the state of affairs, to be laid before a meeting of the shareholders. At a meeting of the directors of the Bank held in Glasgow on 5 October the solicitors reported that although they had at that stage only been able to examine the books very superficially they were already satisfied it was impossible for it to continue in business and they advised a winding up. They further recommended that a meeting of the shareholders should be convened under the provisions of the Companies Acts so that a resolution of liquidation could be passed.

An extraordinary general meeting of the shareholders was thus called for 22 October and on 18 October the solicitors and accountant issued a joint report which made Glasgow gasp. The Bank had lost, on a moderate and probably favourable estimate, £6,200,000, that is the whole of the paid up capital and reserve fund together with fully £5 million besides. Let William Wallace describe the scene:

'. . . there was something like consternation amongst the anxious crowds who besieged the offices of the various newspapers. Men were taken aghast and could not realise the astounding facts disclosed. Nothing like it had been anticipated even by the most pessimistic and groups of haggard and anxious people lounged about the streets until a late hour talking over the dreadful disclosures, while general gloom and an uneasy feeling prevailed.'

The report made it very clear that a loss of this kind would not have happened but for reckless mismanagement in the first place and then deliberate fraud, over a period of years, designed to hide that mismanagement. Accounts had been deliberately falsified, securities entered at fictitious values, bad debts taken as good assets, and the gold which ought to have been held under the Act of 1845 against the notes issued had been squandered to the extent of more than £300,000. 'The Government,' says William Wallace, 'had been deceived by false returns, the shareholders by cooked balance sheets, and everything done, in short, that a perverse ingenuity could think of to conceal the bankrupt condition of the Bank until it became a national calamity.' Hundreds of thousands, it appeared, had been lent to concerns which had promptly gone into liquidation or run off with the proceeds. The writers of the report particularly condemn the Bank for investing in American railway stocks, buying land in Australia and

New Zealand and 'generally behaving like an insane gambler mad to be rid of his fortune'.

William Wallace, in his vigorous language, summed up the conclusions of the report :

'They had lent rather freely on a bad security, or had puffed up some possibly shrewd and rich but over-eager speculator, to the loss of the concern. Then courage failed them; they dared not tell the truth. It was easier to hide losses in ambiguous balance sheets, good only for deception, and the first losses were thus concealed. Then worse came, and it became necessary to go from one criminal act to another in order to keep the ever-increasing losses out of sight, until at last the criminality reached the point of paying a splendid dividend and issuing a balance sheet showing a large surplus, at the very time when the funds of the Bank were so utterly exhausted that the managers had to extract the gold held against the notes in order to keep the concern above water for a few more days. Recklessness led to difficulties and difficulties led to fraud in order that the true state of matters might be kept from the shareholders and the public. As the deposits of honest men came in they were handed over to speculators whose losses daily demanded more and more. One evil step led to another. The utter, almost inconceivable rottenness of the concern had to be cloaked with a fair seeming, and to that end dividends were paid, and when people, perhaps with some suspicion that all was not right, took their stock into the market, it was bought by the bank itself, in order to keep up the quoted price. From first and last there was not one redeeming feature.'

At that time companies were allowed to hold their own stock and when the crash came the Bank held no less than £153,536 of its own stock.

On the publication of the report intense indignation was also expressed when it was disclosed that those directors of the Bank who were most active in its management had failed to show confidence in its future by any large shareholdings : the largest of these was only £1,800 and the smallest £900. Indeed the shareholding of the complete Glasgow Board, which was entrusted with the general management of the Bank, amounted to only £7,300.

Of the other shareholders the largest proportion of the total of 1,272 had shareholdings of only between £200 and £500 (455), while 240 had shareholdings of between £500 and £1,000. Well over 300 had holdings of under £200 and only four had holdings exceeding £10,000. Further, a fifth of the whole number of stockholders held amounts of £100 or under. They represented, as William Wallace rightly says, 'for the most part, people with small savings, the accumulations, perhaps of years of toil, which at one fell swoop were swept away. More than half of the whole number had less than £500 of stock and they were largely people not able to bear any great pressure.'

The report and the outcry it set up were not to be denied. On 19 October 1878 warrants were issued for the arrest of Robert Salmond, Lewis Potter, John Innes Wright, William Taylor, John Stewart and Henry Inglis, all directors; R. S. Stronach, Director and Manager; and Charles Leresche, Secretary.

The complaint by the Procurator-Fiscal on which they were arrested stated that by reason of 'culpable, reckless and fraudulent trading and mismanagement' the Bank was 'in a state of hopeless insolvency and unable to meet its liabilities' and that this insolvency was well-known to the directors or at least some of them five years before the final collapse and that they had 'wickedly and feloniously steal and theftuously away take the . . . several bills of exchange, for sums amounting in all to £23,693. 11. 7d. . . . and did endorse and make over the said several bills of exchange before they had become due to the London Joint-Stock Bank, London, in order that the proceeds thereof might be credited to the City of Glasgow Bank in account between them and the said London Joint-Stock Bank.'

The trial opened on Monday 28 January 1879 in the

presence of a crowded and expectant court. Bail had been denied the accused, so they had languished in prison for over three months. They were arraigned on three main counts which did not materially differ from the original complaint. These were that the directors and officers had fabricated and falsified balance sheets, that some of the directors had availed themselves of their position to obtain advances from the Bank and embezzled the proceeds and that they had stolen bills of exchange which had been sent to them for collection and had used them for paying off debts incurred by the Bank.

However, the opening of the trial was preceded by a discussion on relevancy and the Lord Justice-Clark expunged the first two indictments from the record which, to say the least, was extremely fortunate for the defendants. If they had been convicted of them they would certainly have received severe sentences and the evidence which emerged incidentally during the course of the trial left a very strong suspicion of their guilt on those charges.

Scores of witnesses were called for the prosecution, many of them accountants. Every one indicated enormous discrepancies between the figures as published in the balance sheets and those appearing in the Bank's ledgers. For example James Muir, a Glasgow accountant, pointed out that in the published sheet 'Deposits at the head office and branches, and balances at the credit of banking correspondents' had been shown in 1866 as amounting to £8,364,056; in the Bank ledgers it was £9,370,273. The balance sheet thus understated deposits to the extent of £1,006,216. Drafts accepted by the Bank were understated to the extent of £973,300 on the balance sheet.

Even more damning, Muir brought out the fact that for the years 1873 to 1878 huge sums were advanced by the Bank to certain directors or to their firms. A company known as John Innes Wright & Co, for example, had received no less than £2,325,000 and Innes Wright himself £8,355. The next largest firm to benefit was Potter, Wilson & Co, Lewis Potter's concern, with £510,700.

In all the directors of the Bank had borrowed, it emerged, a total of £3,450,276 and in a single year (1873) the borrowings amounted to a quarter of the whole amount lent by the Bank, a total of £1,339,348 from an overall lending of £4,402,659. Given in detail—Muir was in the box for well over six hours—this kind of evidence was bad enough but worse was to follow when the prosecution called various employees of the Bank and it emerged that all sorts of illogical and inexplicable entries in the books were made to the instructions of the directors.

Following the evidence of William Morison, the chief accountant to the Bank, C. S. Leresche, the Secretary was called. Leresche was arraigned originally with the directors but the charges were subsequently dropped. Leresche's evidence did comparatively little harm to his colleagues although it soon became apparent that the Bank had displayed a wonderful casualness in making advances on property on the other side of the earth, mainly in New Zealand or Australia, without anything approaching proper investigation.

John Turnbull, who had been cashier to the Bank for about 18 years and had been in the Bank's service since 1843 told how the London credit houses had begun to refuse the City of Glasgow Bank's bills early in 1878. This refusal necessitated gold being sent to London. For example, during the week ending 5 January 1878 £60,000 had been sent and then Turnbull falsified the entries to the extent of £60,000 because by law the Bank was required to have gold to cover the issue of notes. False returns continued throughout the whole of the spring and summer of 1878 and towards the end of September amounted to £293,182. For these falsifications Turnbull put the onus fair and square on Robert Stronach, the Manager, and said that the other directors were not aware of the discrepancies until after the Bank had closed.

A number of commercial witnesses were called to give evidence about advances made without due security. John Fleming, for example, a partner in the firm of Smith, Fleming & Co, trading with India, and which had been put into liquidation following a petition of the Solicitor-General after the failure of the Bank, described how until 1870 his firm's indebtedness to the Bank, amounting to about £150,000 had been fully covered by security. Then Smith, Fleming & Co got into difficulties and decided to stop trading. But they were persuaded not to do so by James Fleming's brother, J. N. Fleming who was a director of the Bank at the time. At the time of the failure advances by the Bank to Smith Fleming amounted to something like £1,900,000, all of which were unsecured. It emerged that in spite of these enormous advances the Bank had never made any close inspection of Smith Fleming's affairs and no examination at all for the last three or four years prior to their closure.

The prosecution's case closed with the evidence of a number of Glasgow merchants, mostly in relation to unsecured loans and bad debts which had not been pursued by the Bank with the vigour that might be expected.

The evidence for the defence was far briefer than that of the prosecution, who had called some 40 witnesses in all. The defence's case was mainly directed towards proving that the various advances made to firms connected with the directors were not 'outside of the usual terms of business'. In this they failed dismally. During the course of the prosecution's evidence considerable criticism had arisen of the Bank's practice of putting bad debts into their suspense account rather than writing it off and showing the results in profit and loss. For the defence Willian M'Kinnon, a chartered accountant in Glasgow was called to say that he considered the suspense account a perfectly good place for bad debts, but he failed to convince even the jury on this point although by now they were becoming considerably bemused by the profusion of figures that were being shot at them.

In his address to the jury the Lord Advocate dealt with the fact that the balance sheet had been consistently written down on both sides. He said :

'A question or two was put in the course of the evidence

which seemed rather to suggest that some reliance was to be placed, on the part of the accused, upon the fact that the manipulation of both sides of the balance sheet resulted in the same figures standing at balance, as capital, reserve fund, and profit and loss. That is no test whatever of the truth or falsity of a balance sheet. The purpose of such a balance sheet or abstract is to disclose honestly to the shareholders and the public the amount of business the Bank is doing, their turn-over, the extent of their transactions; and it must be obvious to you that they might have altered the balance sheet by six or eight millions more, by taking that sum off both sides, with precisely the same result of leaving those figures standing at balance as information to the public. But would that have been a right and proper thing to do—to suggest that the Bank was carrying on a business of precisely half the extent with precisely half the amount of money got upon deposit with which they were entrusted? . . . I rather think that when you come to examine into details you will find that the general purpose of representing that the bank was doing a much smaller trade than it really was doing in money, was coupled with this, that it was also intended and calculated to represent they were doing a much better and a much sounder trade than they actually had. Because they diminished the amount of their liabilities by cutting off large sums—in this case we are always dealing with large sums, nothing short of hundreds of thousands and millions—on both sides of the account; and thus they put out of sight an enormous quantity of bill trans-actions which give a clue to the public, who knew in a general way the amount of the dealings of some whom I shall call the leading customers of the bank—the gentlemen who ab-sorbed a great deal of its capital from 1870 onwards, and who, at the time the Bank stopped, had had advanced to them about three-fifths of the whole money the bank had lent. That was one object gained; but in order to keep the two sides of the accounts square they had to diminish the assets—that is to say, what they held in the shape of debts due to them and in the shape of investments and other securities. And how

is that side of the account dealt with? Of course, at first it
looks a very innocent thing to reduce assets; for this is done
in order to preserve the balance on the two sides of the
account . . .'

The Lord Advocate dealt acidly with the Bank's specu-
lations in Australian stock, which he said were undertaken
recklessly to recoup their deficits on other transactions. He
further maintained that the dividends paid bore no relationship whatsoever to the true state of affairs. He dealt also in
detail with the unsecured advances to Morton and Company,
Smith Fleming and Company and James Nicol Fleming
himself—a total of £4,046,000 which he suggested were in
themselves quite sufficient to account for the insolvency of the
Bank. The sum total of his indictment was gross commercial
incompetence, a partiality on the part of the directors to help
themselves and their friends to borrow money from the Bank
of which there was no reasonable hope of repayment; and,
when things inevitably got sticky, of deliberate misrepresent-
ation to cover up the true situation.

The burden of the defence was that here was a storm in a
teacup : 'owing to the wide publicity and misery which had
attended the stoppage of the Bank, public clamour, sometimes
unreasonable, but always powerful, had at once raised its cry
for immediate vengeance and execution of sentence against
those who were believed to be the authors of that misfortune,
without waiting to hear what might legitimately and forcibly
be said in their defence.'

Most of the defendants had separate advocates and each
of them arose in turn to suggest that on the evidence their
clients should be acquitted. None of the defending counsel
argued that the balance sheets were incorrect—reading the
proceedings of the trial one has a feeling that most of them
were rather at sea in the face of the financial evidence—but
they all argued that their particular client had no knowledge
of the falsification. The Dean of Faculty, a Mr Fraser, was
particularly eloquent, as indeed he needed to be, on behalf

of Robert Stronach. He complained bitterly of the conduct
of the prosecution in bringing charges of embezzlement and
theft against the directors and then withdrawing them 'after
they had served their purpose'. Under Scottish law at the time
it was not possible to obtain bail on these charges and 'needless
imprisonment of the directors' had prevented counsel getting
at the facts of the case or learning, until they heard the figures
from the accountant for the Crown, what was the misstate-
ment of which they were accused.

Fraser represented Stronach as a clerk jumped up to
directorship when his brother, who had formerly been a
director, had retired owing to illness. Robert was asked to
take his place, and did so apparently from fraternal affection
rather than from love of office. But he 'steadfastly refused to
advance a sixpence on his own responsibility'. On the account
of falsification of the balance sheets it was argued that Stronach had no knowledge that they were cooked for the purposes
of fraud.

The Lord Justice-Clark's address to the jury was, it was
generally agreed, extremely fair. On the issue of the advances
he said :

'Great mercantile success necessarily produces great mercantile transactions. Where you have merchants who count their
profits by a hundred thousand pounds a year they, of course,
must have the same banking facilities that a man requires who
only counts them by thousands. The proportion will be larger,
but the nature of them will be precisely the same; and it cannot be doubted that a bank that secures for its customers
persons in that enormous scale of business also secures for its
shareholders unusually large profits. But then, gentlemen,
with the magnitude of the transactions there comes a magnitude of danger also, for the merchant, although on that large
scale, is subject, of course, to those fluctuations that have the
effect of tying up a man's money temporarily, and depriving
him of the use of it that he expected, and for these temporary
occasions, of course, a millionaire, as well as the poorer mer-

chant, requires or requests from those with whom he does the
monetary transactions temporary assistance, and he gets it,
with security that if reckoned to be, and if properly valued at,
quite sufficient to keep the bank safe. But then, gentlemen,
comes the crash. A war, a famine, a drought, a strike may
make the whole of that edifice tumble down. The debt and
the security go together. What is the bank to do? Then it is
that the unprofessional director finds himself face to face with
an emergency which, beyond all question, it is difficult and
hard to meet. The question for him then is, is he to bring
the bank down by bringing down the debtor, or is he to carry
on the debtor in the hope of the vessel getting into calmer
water and righting herself in a smoother sea?'

On the subject of the fabrication of the balance sheets he
had this to say :

'Now, what the prosecutor has undertaken to prove, and
says that he has proved, is not that these directors were bound
to know the falsity of the statements in the balance sheet—
not that they lay under obligations to know it, not that they
had the means of knowledge—but that, in point of fact they
did know it; and that is what you must find before you can
convict the prisoners of any part of the offences attributed to
them. You must be able to affirm in point of fact, not that
they had a duty and neglected it, not that they had the means
of information within their power and failed to use them, but
that, as a matter of fact, when that balance sheet was issued
they knew the statements contained in it were false.'

Finally on the issue of intent or motive, the preparation of
a balance sheet to be used fraudulently, he had this to say :

'It is said to have been issued and circulated for the purpose
of deceiving the shareholders and the public as to the true
state of the Bank. Of that you must also be satisfied; but it
would be of no moment that these statements were not in

themselves accurate unless they were put there for a fraudulent and dishonest purpose. It may be suggested that the end which the directors intended to serve was not to injure anyone; that their real object was in the meantime to keep the Bank afloat, until better times should relieve their securities and their debtors, and enable them to pay their way. Gentlemen, I have to tell you that, so far from that being a sufficient defence, it is exactly the offence and the motive described in the indictment, because if they intended to give the Bank breathing time by inducing the shareholders to imagine it was more prosperous than it was, then that is precisely the intent to deceive which is libelled in the indictment, for they put in hazard exactly the same interests which would have been imperilled if they have been actuated by the strongest and most malignant motive. The men who were induced to hold on and the men who were induced to buy are just ruined precisely as they would have been if that had been the result intended by the directors. Did they mean to deceive? If they meant to represent the Bank as being in a more prosperous condition than it was, and if they meant the shareholders to believe that, then they intended to run the risk of all the results that follow from that deception.'

The jury were out for a little under two hours and unanimously found Lewis Potter and Robert Stronach guilty of three charges of falsifying and fabricating the balance sheets of the Bank. John Stewart, Robert Salmond, William Taylor, Henry Inglis and John Innes Wright were found guilty, not of fabricating or falsifying the balance sheets, but of uttering and publishing them, knowing them to be false.

Lewis Potter and Robert Stronach were imprisoned for a period of 18 calendar months. Sentencing them the Lord Justice-Clark said 'I am desirous to say that, as the case now stands, the act which was done by both of you did not necessarily involve, and probably was not actuated by, any design or desire of personal advantage, but was a criminal act commited, as you thought, for the benefit of the Bank. That

c

does not remove it from the category of crime—very far from it—but it does remove from the crime of which you have been convicted the element, as I have said, of corrupt personal motives for personal ends. That consideration has weighed with the court in the sentence . . .'

Sentencing the remainder of the defendants the Lord Justice-Clark said 'We have considered also your case, and looking to the crime of which you have been convicted, and the distinction that may be drawn between you and the other two prisoners, and considering that you have been in jail now since the month of October, the sentence of this court is that you be further imprisoned for eight calendar months.'

During the course of the trial three of the bank officials, Morrison, the accountant; Morris, a private clerk; and Turnbull, who gave false gold returns to the Inland Revenue, had been severely censured but no charges were laid against them.

Following the sentences a wind of indignation swept through Scotland because of their lightness when compared with the financial losses involved. Almost immediately a spate of bankruptcies began, sparked off by the failure of the Bank. But looked at coolly from the distance of almost a century it is difficult to convict the directors of downright criminality although they were certainly guilty of negligence in the conduct of their affairs so serious as to amount to criminal negligence. Unprofessional in their approach, too easily swayed by the demands of their business acquaintances, they lived for at least six years in a sort of wonderland, always hoping that something would turn up to get them out of the situation in which their foolishness had placed them. But it must be remembered that the original charges of embezzlement and theft were withdrawn by the prosecution and the Lord Justice-Clark directed to find the defendants not guilty on these charges.

But even if their motives were the best Stronach and Potter were certainly guilty of deliberate fraud. It is quite likely that the others were merely bad at their sums, although this is a poor qualification for a bank directorship. On much of the evidence one is inclined to take this lenient view but for a fact which is less easy to explain : they were very precise about the monies which they managed to advance to themselves and their interests.

Certainly the *Scots Law Times*, writing as recently as 1930, was not inclined to give them the benefit of the doubt. It said :

'The wrongous actings of the accused and convicted men caused widespread ruin and misery all over the country, some of the effects being felt to this day, and yet the sentences imposed varied from 18 months to eight months imprisonment.'

The Great Railroad Crash

Pennsylvania Central
1845-1970

WHEN ROLLS-ROYCE crashed the City held its
breath. Would it be 1929 all over again?
There was much the same reaction in the States
when Penn Central, 'the huge, filthy, unpunctual, loss-making
. . . railroad system, which serves 103 million customers spread
across 16 of the richest and most industrialised of the Eastern
United States' went bankrupt in 1970. As Peter Wilsher of the
Sunday Times Business News recorded at the time, 'This was
a major financial collapse by any standards and the world's
stock markets gave a couple of sickening, convulsive heaves
before agreeing . . . to digest the news without panic.'

Penn Central had been around, in one form or another,
for a long time. But it was one of the first victims, and
certainly by far the largest, of the Wall Street slump of 1970
and—many Americans argue—of Nixon's control policies on
money and credit. This is partially true—the state of the
economy was the final straw which toppled Penn Central, but
it also seems that the disaster was the final outcome of bad
management on a very large scale for many years.

Penn Central as it existed until 1970 was the product of the
biggest merger in industrial history and was put together in
January 1968 from the ailing remains of two of the most

famous of all the US railroads, the New York Central and the Pennsylvania which, historically, had been competitors for over 100 years. Then, at the end of 1968, they were joined by the already bankrupt New Haven Railway so that finally they had a staff of just under 100,000, a payroll of nearly $1,000 million a year, about 4,200 locomotives and 180,000 passenger coaches and trucks—the largest railway conglomerate in the world.

Penn Central is something which is deep in the American blood, just like Rolls-Royce in Britain although in the case of Penn Central it is often considered a scourge on the face of the earth it covers. As Peter Wilsher said at the time it had succeeded in earning a reputation 'for managerial inefficiency which gives British Rail the appearance of being covered with rose petals and good housekeeping awards'.

Instead of the merger resulting in the streamlining of operations and an elimination of duplication, the troubles of the two railroads were compounded. Both the goods and passenger services, already poor, became chaotic. The filthy trains arrived hours late. Derailments became a commonplace, mainly because years of deferred maintenance took their toll in the end. Just before the financial crash the once-proud 'Spirit of St Louis', a crack train, ran habitually one to three hours late because of bad track and repair work. Throughout 1969 and 1970 officers of the company promised a special maintenance programme to bring the main lines back to normal by the autumn. By then it was too late; Penn Central had collapsed.

Penn's problems, and indeed those of the whole railroad system in the States, go back to the end of the war. Different companies covered the same territory and were forced to fight tooth and nail for business; the rates they could charge for passenger services were controlled by the Government and were usually at least two steps behind current inflation. Also, in the Eastern States particularly, the Government had opened up the waterways during the war and these, coupled with better roads and price cutting road hauliers brought the freight carried down to levels lower than before the first world war. Throughout the 50's the Penn Central conglomerate (then two railroads) was earning less than 1% on its enormous capital.

For all the US railroads during this period debts mounted steadily; nervous breakdowns and ulcerated executives became commonplace. Robert Ralph Young, at one time President of New York Central had big ideas and then, as the great mountain of problems wore him down, committed suicide.

The idea of combining New York Central and Pennsylvania was a government brainchild dating back to 1957. It took over 10 years to accomplish. In the first place the two railroads were hereditary competitors, 'The dirtiest men in the business,' as a New York Central indoctrinated engine driver said of a Pennsylvania conductor. And no doubt the Pennsylvania men thought the same or even worse. Then the whole issue had to go before an Interstate Commerce Commission which had to plough through a 160 inch thick pile of objections from the public. American commentators have said that these delays cost the railroad system a billion dollars.

Theoretically the merger when it was finally accomplished should have worked very well. Both railroads were built up to serve the most prosperous area of the most prosperous country in the world. Waste, such as the $150 million which each of them spent every year collecting stray freight wagons from the other's territories would be saved; duplicate lines could be torn up; duplicate buildings closed down; staff commitments reduced. Peter Wilsher has quoted *Fortune Magazine* as saying in 1965:

'Few exercises exhilarate the financial world more than speculating what the Pennsylvania New York Central transportation company will be doing in ten years if the great plans now being laid for the system come to fruition'.

Well at least *Fortune* left it open, which is just as well because in their August 1970 issue the major article was on the Penn Central bankruptcy express.

In 1968, the merger completed, shares of Penn Central were quoted on the New York Stock Exchange at 84 and Stuart T. Saunders, formerly President at Pennsylvania and the Group's first Chief Executive was enthusiastically voted in the *Saturday Review Poll* as 'Businessman of the Year'.

Less than two years later the same shares were down to 34 —and at the time of the debacle had fallen to $7\frac{1}{2}$. Saunders, together with his Vice-Chairman, Alfred Perlman who was President of New York Central until the merger, the finance committee Chairman and seven other top executives were fired by the main Board. In 1968 the new Penn Central had a profit of $87.8 million; in 1969 it dropped to $4.4 million. Halfway through 1970 when the crash came losses for the year were already well in excess of $30 million.

But Penn Central, like most railways, had a number of important side interests. If the railroad activities are taken alone—and after all that is what they were in business for— there were losses of $56.3 million in 1969 and at the time of the crash it was estimated that they were losing some $700,000 a day on freight and passenger services combined.

Rising costs, a 7% wages settlement, the stagnation of US economic activity and accrued maintenance bills have all been blamed.

Before the two companies merged they had spent around $2,500 million on improvements from 1960-8. Since that date and until the collapse another $600 million was put into the system. The truth is that the whole thing became just too big for human brains to comprehend and the computer system, supposed to be used for the tracking of wagons, was no more successful. As shipments arrived damaged, weeks late, or not at all, the few customers remaining faithful to Penn Central took their business elsewhere.

Increasingly during the last two years of its life executives of Penn Central had to spend time not in trying to make the railroad more efficient—an enormous job in itself—but in increasing their frantic attempts to raise money. Borrowing, re-borrowing, mortgaging, re-mortgaging, Eurodollar loans, the lot. As one top executive said : 'I came here because of my experience of running railroads. Now I reckon I could run a bank.'

It was the final failure to raise a $100 million debenture (to add to the $2,600 million the company already owed), the depressed Wall Street market, and the refusal of the House Banking Committee to endorse a move whereby the Pentagon would be able to guarantee a $200 million loan on the grounds that Penn Central was vital to national security, that brought on the crash.

A small army of accountants and attorneys are still sorting out the precise situation in relation to Penn Central. Officially it was the transportation company which ran the railroad that went into bankruptcy and the situation of the subsidiary concerns which own hotels and a great deal of very valuable urban property, including almost the whole of New York's Park Avenue between Grand Central Station and the Manufacturers Hanover Trust Building, are separate problems. Estimates of what it will take to really put Penn Central on its feet again vary from $500 to $1,000 million.

By Friday 19 June 1970 and to quote *Fortune* again, 'The Penn Central Transportation Company rolled towards bankruptcy with the finality of an express train thundering through the night. The railroad had run out of cash. Virtually every asset it owned was either mortgaged or pledged and the banking community was not making any more loans—not without a Government guarantee. In terms of assets ($4.6 billion) it was the biggest bankruptcy in history.'

Many observers believe that the merger could never have worked and was the sole reason for Penn's downfall. If this is so they kept remarkably quiet at the time, although with the benefit of hindsight it is possible to pinpoint all sorts of differences, of attitude and approach, of personnel and of operating styles.

The Pennsylvania got much of its business by hauling steel, ore and coal while the Central was founded on moving merchandise from the factories of the Mid-West to the consumers of the North-East. Thus the Pennsylvania depended on volume but New York Central offered speed and service. The Pennsylvania has been described as a 'massive bureaucracy that worked on a strict military chain of command'; the Central under Alfred E. Perlman was known for some of its highly unconventional methods and for the entrepeneurial brilliance of Perlman himself. One can be forgiven for wondering how the two top men, Stuart T. Saunders on the one hand, a lawyer and a politician, and flamboyant Perlman on the other, an operational railroader all his life, hit it off. Perlman, operation-orientated all his life was always specific, always detailed in his approach. Saunders on the other hand rarely visited the railroads themselves and believed in broad orders which his executives must implement in detail or be fired. Both men were known for their tempers. Perlman, says *Fortune,* 'was a fearsome antagonist, for he could cut down a man with a sarcasm that sliced like a frozen scalpel.' But Saunders 'punctuated his threats with a growing temper that started with a crimson tide that swept up over his face and across his round dome.'

Critics say that the whole merger situation was mishandled when it was decided that, as soon as legally joined, the two companies should begin operating as one. So routes were changed immediately for some types of traffic and because none of the classification clerks had been taught the 5,000 new combinations of routings, trucks started flowing by the thousands into the wrong yards. Soon yards were jammed and trains were unable to get in. Many trains had no waybills at all and yard superintendents were sending out entire trains with no waybills just to get rid of them, thus making more confusion at the next station down the line. Whole trains became lost for days; in one case, at the end of 1968, a coal train of more than 100 trucks was lost for 10 days outside Syracuse.

This was a terrible case of management failing to work in unison or to communicate. Perlman was loyal to his old New York Central team and Saunders protected the interests of his

Pennsylvania men. Generally a department was headed by a former Pennsylvania man, followed by a Central man, followed by a Pennsylvania man and so on down the line. Chaos resulted.

Saunders's method of management, perform-or-be-fired, was directly counter to Perlman's technique of leading men by encouraging them. Perlman, too, was very soon a frustrated man because, used to complete control over his own company, he had no say in the finances of Penn Central.

Disagreement after disagreement finally led to Perlman's resignation, which Saunders accepted, probably with alacrity. Perlman took the meaningless job of Vice-Chairman, of which he was relieved shortly before the bankruptcy. Paul A. Gorman, 62, then President of Western Electric, was appointed in his place. At least Gorman was neutral and he reorganised top management, reducing the number of Vice-Presidents who reported directly to him and also replacing some of those executives who just wouldn't work with their opposite numbers for the good of the new Penn Central.

In the save or bust operation that was now mounted another key man was Mike Flannery who had been one of Perlman's operating officers at the Central. In the autumn of 1969 he did a great deal to reduce chaos on the tracks. Then he was hit with the worst winter in living memory. In New England, in particular, miles of lines were torn up by frost and locomotives were frozen up all over the system. Even so, when the crash came they still had enormous problems, daily getting worse because of maintenance deferred because of the chronic cash shortage.

Many observers believe that, quarrels apart, Penn Central was killed by the optimism of Saunders on one side and Perlman's negative thinking on the other. For example, Saunders stated that the 1969 operating deficit was caused solely by the railroads' passenger losses but in fact they amounted to only half the true total deficit.

Due to what has been described as 'some unique book-keeping' the parent Penn Central company was able to report very happy profits, which lulled creditors, shareholders, directors and managers. The Companies Auditors received more than $600,000 for accounting services in its last year and these Company accounts were accepted by the Interstate Commerce Commission, which is charged with keeping an eye on the finances of the US's railways. Nevertheless, it is a fact that such normal operating expenses as wages were taken out of capital rather than income, thus inflating Penn Central's reported profits by millions of dollars. *Fortune* says that some bills for fright charges, which were reportedly uncollectable, were credited to income. Sales of real estate, which should have been designated as extraordinary items or the sale of capital assets, were credited to normal income and so were the profits from security sales. Assets were also written off as extraordinary charges to avoid annual depreciation, and thus earnings were enhanced. When a large block of securities was exchanged the paper profit from the transaction was credited to normal income in instalments over the following years—but no cash was ever received by the company. In some transactions the railroad company sold assets to its financial subsidiary at many times their book value and credited the difference to its own income as profit. Then the railroad fed its own capital into affiliated companies and took it back in the form of dividends—some of which, it is alleged, were very high.

Rush Loving Junior and other American financial commentators assert that these accounting practices disguised the true state of affairs from even informed financial circles. Although Penn Central told its shareholders that it earned $4,400,000 before extraordinary items in 1969 Loving says it actually suffered a normal loss of at least $95 million and it may have lost as much as $120 million. Even after an extraordinary gain of $18 million from the sale of securities the loss was more than $75 million. As already indicated, reported earnings also included $8 million in unpaid freight bills and unkind critics say that in many cases the railroad did not know who to send the bills to, having lost the records. When the bankrupt New Haven Railroad was acquired it cost Penn Central $22 million to modernise its equipment and this was taken from capital rather than from operating expenses.

In 1969 Penn Central received some very satisfactory dividends from subsidiary interests, including real estate and coal companies. At the same time, however, Penn Central was making loans to these same subsidiaries from its own capital. The dividends boosted Penn Central's earnings by $35 million and $19 million of this amount was received from five companies. But directly or through subsidiaries Penn Central advanced the same five companies at least $17,300,000.

The source of these dividends has also been questioned. Penn Central, for example, owns the New York Central Transport Company which had a 1969 profit of only $4,200,000; yet Penn Central's accounts showed a $14,500,000 dividend from the same company. Another subsidiary, Merchants Despatch Transportation Corporation showed a $2,800,000 profit for 1969 but paid Penn Central a $4,700,000 dividend. There were several other cases of this kind.

Fortune has contended that while Penn Central reported a profit of $90 million for 1968 they actually had a loss of more than $20 million. The company had a $54 million gain from security sales but listed this as normal income instead of sales of assets. In capitalising the merger costs which occurred that year earnings were increased by $23,800,000.

In 1968 the railroad also included in its profits a dividend of $11,700,000 which was in fact merely a property exchange. It represented Penn Central's interest in Union Station, Washington, which was transferred during the year from the Washington Terminal Company to Terminal's two owners, Penn Central and the Baltimore and Ohio Railroad. Penn Central based the dividend on the price it expected to get for the station when it was sold to the US Department of the Interior as a visitors' centre. In fact the sale had still not been completed at the date of the failure.

Always the object seemed to be to create confidence and

assure bankers, shareholders and the public that Penn could meet its commitments.

Since the event Saunders has come in for some very heavy criticism for maintaining an unrealistic dividend policy. For example, in 1968 Penn had a $300 million programme of capital expenditure with only about $100 million available. Despite this the shareholders were voted $55 million.

Since the crash some of the directors have been busy telling the American press that they were not aware of the company's real financial position but early in 1969 Murray A. Harding, a Wall Street analyst, pointed out that Penn Central's 1968 earnings had been inflated by the Washington Union Station 'dividend'. Nevertheless a further dividend was voted for the first quarter of 1969 although by mid-year the affairs of the company had deteriorated so obviously that David C. Bevan, the chairman of the finance committee, recommended that dividend payments be halted. But Saunders was intent on good shareholder relations and decided the payout should continue. He pointed out that he was trying to build Penn Central into a conglomerate and the dividend payout would hold up the company's price-earnings ratio. Since that date Saunders is reported to have realised his mistake and he thinks that dividends were paid for too long. However, when the autumn dividend came up for consideration the company was having great difficulty in finding the cash to meet its wages, let alone its creditors, and there was no dividend for the shareholders. But in two very difficult years with the cash flow drying up all the time nearly $100 million had been paid to Penn Central's shareholders.

All this time Bevan had been forced to borrow to keep the company in business. In 1968 the Eurodollar market had provided $50 million as a short-term loan. In 1969 he got a further $50 million in 'revolving credit' and raised $85 million more from bond and debenture sales. At the end of 1969 with the situation getting ever more difficult he borrowed another $59 million for the year from Europe at a terrifying interest rate of 10.1%.

Then the bad winter weather hit the company and in the year ahead (1970) it had to meet $106 million in sinking fund requirements. Bevan was driven to mortgage nearly everything the company possessed. He also sold $193,400,000 in unsecured commercial paper. Yet the winter alone set the company back around $100 million.

In February 1970 Bevan went off to New York to negotiate yet another loan while Saunders headed a deputation to the Interstate Commerce Commission. This commission regulates the freight and passenger rates and Saunders asked for an increase for the whole country, to be granted immediately. The move seems to indicate a certain failure on Saunders's part, even then, to face reality. A freight rate increase that would still keep the business in the railroad's hands wouldn't by that time have had a chance of saving Penn Central. In March Saunders also explained the situation to the US Secretary of Transportation and in April and May a scheme was worked out for Federal guarantees of Penn Central loans. There were also talks with the Defence Department, presumably on the grounds that Penn Central was considered a strategic necessity.

Meanwhile Bevan put together a $100 million debenture to be sold in late May or early June so that the railroad might meet its sinking fund requirement. At first Wall Street seemed to be quite favourably inclined towards the debenture but in late April when Penn Central announced the first quarter's losses, made worse by the winter, Wall Street reacted immediately and unfavourably. Penn Central found it was unable to sell the debentures to refinance the stock that was becoming due for payment.

In May Saunders was in Washington for a meeting with the Secretary of the Treasury, David M. Kennedy. If, said Saunders, he could not get guarantees for further loans the railroad subsidiary, Penn Central Transportation Company, would have to consider filing for bankruptcy within the next few days. Kennedy was both stunned and alarmed. With the stock market in its state of decline news of the bankruptcy of

Penn Central might trigger off a chain reaction, if not an outright panic. Moreover, if Penn Central collapsed it would bring heavy losses to many of the nation's big mutual funds. Administration leaders hurriedly prepared a $200 million immediate Defence Department guarantee for Penn Central and drew up a bill to guarantee another $750 million in railroad loans generally, a large proportion of which was designated for Penn. Meanwhile, on Monday 8 June an internal showdown took place when the other directors threw out Saunders, Bevan and Perlman.

The next day the Administration leaders briefed congressional leaders and asked for support of the proposed bill to guarantee $750 million in railroad loans. Congressman Wright Patman vigorously opposed such guarantees and questioned also the legality of the interim $200 million guarantee. Other congressional members were cool and by the following week, that bill was as good as dead.

The Defence Department guarantee was still left but this would only give enough to Penn Central to get it through the summer. It might be a question of throwing good money after bad if the company still went bankrupt when the money ran out around 1 October. At this point the Administration were faced with a situation not so very different from that which the British Government were to face in relation to Rolls-Royce a year later. Should they push out more money in guarantees or should they let the company go to the wall, risking a slide in the stock market, and perhaps many other bankruptcies and even panic? The US Administration made the same choice as the British Government were to do a few months afterwards. On Friday 19 June it withdrew its support.

That night the executive committee of the directors met in Philadelphia. Over $30 million in loans were to come due by the end of the month, nearly $2 million of them on Monday and there was virtually no cash in the till. Paul A. Gorman, who had so recently been catapulted into Saunders's seat, recommended voluntary bankruptcy, as quickly as possible, before the banks moved in and filed petitions against them.

By going the voluntary route Penn Central could ask for an orderly reorganisation while the other method meant chaos and possible liquidation.

On the Sunday morning Gorman met the full Board and asked for authority to file a bankruptcy petition. The meeting dragged on for hours because by then the whole matter had gone to the White House. They waited until 5.35 in the afternoon then decided to file. Judge Kraft who had been standing by, signed the bankruptcy order.

Not surprisingly the bankruptcy set off a multitude of hearings, investigations and law suits. In February 1971, for example, Mr Maurice Stans, the Secretary of Commerce was charged by Congress that he was guilty of improper behaviour in not revealing shareholdings worth about $300,000 in a Penn Central subsidiary. Mr Stans vigorously denied the allegation.

Just as in the case of Rolls-Royce confusion ensued about associated companies. The railroad company was in bankruptcy but what was the situation in relation to its parent, the Penn Central Company and its subsidiary, the Pennsylvania Company? It turned out that Pennsylvania Company was actually a subsidiary of the railroad and its common stock was pledged against railroad loans. The parent Penn Central Company, it emerged, in fact owned only two small oil companies as assets and since the bankruptcy their former owners have sued for their return. On top of that the holding company had guaranteed the railroad's $59 million Swiss loan. Thus Penn Central's investors were left with virtually nothing and among the shareholders were more than 7,000 Penn Central employees, many of whom not only faced the risk of going unpaid but also of losing their jobs. Saunders was reported to have borrowed heavily to acquire 45,000 shares in the railroad but payment of his $114,000 pension, voted by the directors after his dismissal, was held up by a Federal court.

Bad management and bad supervision of management appears to have been the major reason for the failure of Penn Central. Saunders and Perlman were poor business mates and their attitude went right down the line. It also seems that all those who were concerned with financial responsibility failed miserably and *Fortune* has asserted that 'the accounting profession as a whole contributed to the debacle by making acceptable practices that are an open invitation to distortions and outright fraud'.

Meanwhile the dilemma of the US railroads continues. In 1971 the Government took over the operation of most passenger trains but this was not sufficient and early in 1972 it was becoming more and more obvious that the nation's whole railroad system was threatened with collapse.

While Penn Central's directors probably deserve all the outspoken criticism they have received in the American press the fact remains that five major rail companies in the States are already bankrupt. The Interstate Commerce Commission listed, in April 1972, another 12 as 'marginal' indicating that they might go bankrupt at any moment. Track all over the country is deteriorating fast—on a national average it is being computed on a basis which means that each rail must last 120 years although in fact it remains serviceable for less than half that time.

Between 1966 and 1970 US derailments doubled to an average of 2,394 a year. Expenditure necessary during the next 10 to 12 years is likely to be in the order of $36 billion.

If management has failed to solve the admittedly heavy problems the trade unions certainly have not helped, and in spite of the penniless circumstances of their employers they strike freely and frequently. The employers are also hampered by rule books which were compiled at the turn of the century. For example, train crews must be paid a full day's wages for every 100 miles travelled—a distance that the fastest diesel locomotives can cover in less than two hours. Some States require trains to carry five-man crews.

Whether the United States like it or not—and the great majority of citizens don't—it is very difficult to see how nationalisation of the railways can be avoided before the end of the decade.

D

Shipbuilding in Slow Decline

C. & W. Earle and their successors 1845-1932

TO THIS DAY, in spite of the vicissitudes which British shipbuilding has suffered in recent years, Hull, on the east coast of Yorkshire, still builds ships—mostly light vessels such as trawlers, tugs and coastal craft.

But in the 19th century it was a large and thriving centre for shipbuilding. In the early part of the century there were a number of shipyards concerned with the building of wooden sailing vessels. Some naval ships were built at the port during the Napoleonic Wars and many were built for the whaling and merchant interests. The first steam packet was built in Hull in 1823 and eight years later an iron steam boat was launched from a yard on the Humber Bank.

In 1845 two brothers, Charles and William Earle took over foundry premises and set up business as 'engineers, millwrights, founders, ship and general smiths'. By 1851 they are on record as employing 72 men and they had acquired a shipyard in Victoria Dock where they launched their first ship in March 1853. This was an iron screw steam ship, *Minister Thorbeck* of 100 gross tons. It was built for the Zwolle Steam Navigation Company, a Dutch concern engaged in coastal trading.

The history of the Earle firm is of particular interest because during its long life it traded in those three forms most common to British commercial organisation: the partnership, the private limited company, and the public company—although, in the case of Earle's not in that order. The partnership existed from 1845-70 when Charles died. The illness of William in the following year made the latter sell the business and it was then converted to a public company in 1871 as Earle's Shipbuilding and Engineering Co Ltd. In 1900, having suffered severe financial difficulties for 10 or more years previously, the company went into voluntary liquidation and the following year a Mr Charles Henry Wilson, a prominent Hull shipowner, took over the business and it was run as a private limited company, owned mainly by members of the Wilson family, until 1932 when it was closed down.

Although Earle's finally collapsed with hardly a whimper, let alone with a resounding crash—unlike many of the other concerns discussed in this book—it was in its time a company of considerable importance. Between 1853 and 1931 nearly 700 ships were built by the firm, great quantities of machinery were supplied to other builders and many ships were extensively repaired in their dockyards. Of the ships built a considerable number supplied were warships and over the years the men at the head of the business ran through pretty well the whole gamut of commercial problems.

In the first years the Earle brothers had difficulty in meeting the demand for shipping created by the development of British overseas trade in the 1840s and, a little later, the outbreak of the Crimean War in 1854. Ships were also getting larger. At the outset the brothers were faced with the problems of expanding quickly with inadequate capital resources and consequent difficulties of cash flow.

However, by and large they prospered. In 1863 they acquired a yard on the bank of the Humber where they were able to launch ships directly into the river. By 1865 their output had risen to over 9,000 gross tons and the opening of the Suez Canal in 1869 stimulated the shipbuilding industry generally so that by 1871 they had an output of 18,900 gross tons. In 1870 they built their largest ship—*Canopus* of 2,800 gross tons for a Liverpool firm.

During the whole period of the partnership a considerable amount of the building was for a single company, the Hull shipowners Thomas Wilson (no connection with the Wilsons who later acquired the business) who placed orders for very nearly 40% of the Earle's output, but this does not seem to have caused any problems. In 1864 they had expanded sufficiently to be employing nearly 2,000 hands.

However, while no very precise records exist of this period, it is doubtful if the Earle brothers had it all their own way. Apart from the competition from other local shipbuilders there were the builders on the rivers Tees, Clyde and Tyne. Nevertheless it seems likely that the Earle partnership was the largest firm of shipbuilders in the area although in the 60s Hull became firmly established as a centre of the steamship building industry.

Expansion meant a need for continually increasing capital. In 1863 the partnership capital was £33,476, of which William had £17,532 and Charles £15,944. Six years later this had risen to just over £99,000 but unfortunately there are no records to show whether this increase in the partnership capital was provided from the partners' personal resources or whether they were able to achieve such an increase by ploughing back profits. However it is known that to provide additional finance they obtained a mortgage of £26,000 on their property from the Corporation of Hull Trinity House in 1864.

Charles Earle died suddenly in 1870 when William was already in ill health. The following year Wiliam decided to negotiate the sale of the business and in August 1871 the last balance sheet, drawn up to the end of the partnership, showed assets of £243,800. So it is evident that in less than 30 years the brothers had built up a substantial business producing nearly 20,000 gross tons of shipping each year. The turnover for the three years prior to the sale had averaged £250,000 per annum.

David Chadwick, a member of parliament and well-known

at the time as a company promoter, bought the business from William Earle—who died a few months later—on behalf of a proposed joint stock company, Earle's Shipbuilding and Engineering Co Ltd. The purchase was at a favourable time; not only had the Suez Canal been opened but Britain was acknowledged as world leader in the use of iron for ship-building.

The public company was launched with an authorised capital of £30,000, divided into 6,000 shares of £50 each and within three days capital was over-subscribed by a cool £150,000. The new company was soon working at full stretch and by 1872 the British shipbuilding industry was prosperous as it had never been before.

The first Chairman and General Manager of the company was Edward J. Reed, first secretary of the Institution of Naval Architects and a former naval architect for the British Navy. During his time in the service he designed iron-clad vessels. Other directors included Sir John Brown, founder of the Shef-field iron and steel firm of that name, Admiral Robinson of London, Thomas Bingham and John Galloway, an engineer from Manchester. Earle's Shipbuilding & Engineering Co Ltd was no longer a local company : the majority of shares were held by merchants, manufacturers and tradesmen, engineers and professional men in London, Sheffield and Manchester.

While the early years of the 70s were successful for the com-pany it suffered heavy losses from about 1875 onwards and did not begin to recover until the end of the decade. The next decade (1880-90) was a period of consolidation and a vigorous and successful attempt was made to secure Admiralty con-tracts. Steel began to be used in shipbuilding and Earle's were one of the pioneers of the new triple expansion engines.

The apparent years of prosperity and a high level of activity following the dissolution of the partnership were misleading. Because of William's illness there were in fact few orders in the yard at the time the business was transferred and the first contracts of the new company were accepted at low prices to prevent laying off labour. Also it seems fairly clear that the

first year's dividend—of 12½%—was far too high. Labour
costs went up steeply in 1873 and profits went down but a
dividend of 12½% was repeated. Another difficulty was that
the new company, led by more ambitious men, was after
large orders for ships of over 3,000 gross tons and many of the
old craftsmen could not handle this work efficiently.

One unprofitable venture in which Earle's became involved
was the Bessemer Saloon Steamer which incorporated an in-
vention based on hydraulics to keep the floor of the cabin perfectly level even when the ship was rolling violently. A company was formed to promote this ship in which Earle's held
6,000 fully paid shares, but the Bessemer was in fact abandoned after a single trial and the Bessemer Company went
into liquidation owing Earle's £17,350. The company was
also involved in the building of two German ships which lost
them a further £40,000 and by 1875 when the extent of the
losses became apparent, low dividends were declared. In fact
at this period things were so bad that Earle's was forced to
sell part of their land.

E. J. Reed, who had been retained at a salary of £5,000 a
year, resigned as General Manager at the end of 1873 and the
following year his Chairmanship was also terminated. His
departure, in view of the financial pressures to which the company was subjected, was not entirely happy and in its annual
report for 1874 the company indicated, in polite terms, that
the directors were in profound disagreement with Mr Reed.
Sir John Brown replaced Reed as chairman of the company
and he admitted that their misfortunes had arisen from taking
too many contracts at prices at which it had obtained work
previously, whereas labour and material had risen at least 35%
over a period of three years. During the latter part of the 70s
the company borrowed heavily from its bankers, the London
and Yorkshire Bank Ltd, and the directors were guaranteeing
overdrafts to the tune of £30,000. Annual increments were
still due to the executors of the Earle brothers and amounted
to around £5,000 a year. The directors considered that this
was 'so impoverishing the concern' that it was decided to pay

off the remaining £27,000 and borrow a further £40,000 on mortgage, interest on which was 5%.

Much of Earle's troubles followed the general depression in shipbuilding in the mid-70s, although some improvement occurred in 1877-8 when they managed to pay dividends of 2½ and 3%. In 1879, however, they were in difficulties again. The depression had hit the shipbuilding industry as a whole once more and Earle's output was the lowest for 18 years. To make matters worse the north-east coast builders around Sunderland were waging a price war and even the local shipowners in Hull forsook their local connections and went north in the search for better prices. At this time there seems to have been a surplus of capital in the Sunderland yards and many of the shipbuilders in this area were not only quoting competitively but offering two or three years credit.

Throughout the whole of the 70s Earle's labour force fluctuated wildly but in 1880 trade began to improve; by the autumn of that year they were employing some 2,200 men and by the end of the year 3,000 had been engaged. They were working then on their first two steel ships and making engines, too. In 1882 the company built the largest vessel they had so far tackled, *Grecian Monarch*, a merchant vessel of 4,260 gross tons. In the same year they also built a cruiser for the Royal Navy and a number of other large merchant ships.

During the early 80s boom conditions generally tempted other shipbuilders to start in Hull and although they were not very successful Earle's were hit with labour difficulties. In 1883 the manager reported that while at least 3,000 men were needed for existing contracts, a weekly average of only 2,346 could be engaged. Worse still, wage rates had been forced up throughout the country because of the labour shortage and the first of the shipbuilding strikes made their destructive influence felt.

Another problem for Earle's was the financing of the large ships which they were building at this period. Also the pattern of commerce in the industry had changed: in the 70s deposits were paid when contracts were signed but 10 years later most work was on an instalment basis, so that money was not received until earned and paid out.

The shipbuilding boom of the early 1880s passed away but Earle's were saved by the triple expansion engine, for which they received many contracts. By 1888 the expansion of this successful engine enabled them to pay off some of their mortgages and in 1888 they paid a 5% dividend although their total capital was less than the assets by about £30,000 and part of the money for the dividend was taken from the reserve fund. About this time, too, they received a number of orders for Admiralty cruisers although they were badly affected by the widespread strikes which took place throughout the country in 1889. Engineers received increased wages as a result of their strike but almost immediately a demarcation dispute followed between the joiners and shipwrights which persisted for 12 weeks.

Nevertheless in 1890 and 1891 profits were £22,000 and £35,000 respectively—the highest in the history of the company. But the directors had learned their lesson and dividend payments were restrained. It was agreed that for a long period insufficient provision had been made for depreciation and expenditure on new machinery and tools had too often been met by relying on the accommodation of the company's bankers and creditors. Greater emphasis was placed on repair work and engine building and it was recognised that the company was unable to compete in the building of tramp steamers, overheads killing the very small profit margins.

During the early 90s the company continued with its now-familiar round of advances and setbacks. During this period it relied very largely on Admiralty orders for cruisers and engines. Some of this work was profitable; other contracts were not and one government order resulted in a loss of £30,000. The long strikes of dockers at Hull during the early part of 1893 and of colliers in the following summer resulted in the company showing a loss of £4,900 and the dividend of 3% paid in 1892 was in fact the last ever to be paid by the public company.

After so many years the work for Wilson's, on which the partners had rested so heavily, declined for the first time. In 1894, following the year when the output sank to the lowest level since the company was formed (only 2,800 gross tons) the Articles of Association were altered to enable the directors to borrow up to two-thirds of the paid-up capital.

Sir John Brown as chairman resigned in 1892 and was succeeded by J. Galloway, the last of the original directors. Galloway held office for only a year but the company's difficulties were so acute that in 1893 he lent £10,000 without security. A prolonged national dispute of engineers in 1897-8 was virtually the death knell of the company. In 1898 a loss of £13,600 was shown, which together with a debit balance from the previous year, due to the loss on the government contracts, resulted in a total loss of £38,600 and the Junction Foundry, which was the original works of the Earle brothers, was sold to the North Eastern Railway Company.

In June 1900 the shareholders agreed on a voluntary liquidation of the company in view of the fact that their bankers refused further advances and creditors were suing for £10,000. Charles Wilson offered to pay £217,500 for the business in December of that year. This would have paid off the debenture holders, certain preferential claims and 6s 8d in the £ to unsecured creditors but there would have been nothing left for the ordinary shareholders. The offer was opposed and an attempt was made to reconstruct the company in order to obtain more working capital to complete existing contracts on a profitable basis, but the plan did not succeed. Earle's were widely canvassed with a view to amalgamation but nobody came forward. Finally Mr Wilson made another offer to purchase in 1900 and this was accepted.

The liquidators of the public company gave permission for the formation of a new company under the same name, to be registered as a private limited company with a capital of £150,000. Charles Wilson, as a director, held the majority of shares and his two sons were also directors. The purchase price was £170,000 and at the end of 1902 the land and property held by the company were mortgaged to the Wilsons for debenture stock of £100,000.

How much the shareholders and creditors received cannot be determined because the winding-up accounts of the old company are no longer available but in 1898 the business had been valued at £402,152 and Charles Wilson purchased for less than half this sum.

The first ship under the new management was launched in 1902 and by 1905 the work force had been built up to 1,900 men. In 1906 when the engineers went on strike in Hull Charles Wilson (or Lord Nunburnholme as he had now become) threatened to close the yard. In his statement he said that he had no intention of working at a loss and that the disputes in the last 20 years of the previous century had ruined the old company. The strike continued for some time but Earle's was able to get non-union labour so that the works were not closed down. Another difficult period was in 1908, one of the worst years in national shipbuilding history, but thereafter output rose steadily, to a peak of 31,200 gross tons in 1914. Wilsons were again large customers and until the first world war 41% of the output went to them, for ships of between 2,000 and 7,000 gross tons.

Lord Nunburnholme died in 1907 and was succeeded by his eldest son, C. H. Wellesley Wilson. The Dowager Lady Nunburnholme was made a director of Earle's in 1917 and in that year the capital was increased to £250,000. In the last years of the company's life ships supplied to local owners declined substantially, although over 50,000 gross tons were produced for the Ellerman Lines, successors to the Wilson's who had been faithful customers ever since the Earle brothers started up business.

During the First World War Earle's achieved the highest working force in their history: nearly 4,000—but by 1920 output had fallen to 10,500 gross tons and reached its lowest ebb in the immediate post-war years. By 1923 the yards produced only 3,400 tons.

However, worse was to come and by 1928 only 500 gross

tons were built. There was a slight recovery in 1929 to 9,300 gross tons but the writing was on the wall and the yard was closed down in June 1932. It was then acquired by the National Shipbuilders Securities Ltd, under the scheme for rationalisation of yards, which precluded its use as a shipbuilding yard for 40 years. The property was put up for sale in 1933 and at the final winding-up meeting of the company the following year the shareholders received only £2 9s per £10 share.

Thus, most undramatically, ended the history of one of the principal shipbuilding yards in Hull, one of the largest single employers of labour in the area and a very considerable training ground for men who subsequently set up business on their own as shipbuilders or makers of engines and boilers. Among the ships built by Earle's were 17 warships for the British Navy, 148 steamers for Wilson's and Ellerman's Wilson, 284 sets of machinery, together with many ships supplied to local, national and foreign owners and extensive repair work both of ships and engines.

While the story of Earle's, unlike others in this book, has no dramatic highlights it is representative of many other companies—yet is unusual too, because, apart from the period when it was a private limited company, its affairs are very well documented and have been preserved for posterity. Some years ago Joyce M. Bellamy of the University of Hull, made an extensive study of this concern and drew together all the documentation in existence, subsequently published in Volume 6 of 'Business History'. I am greatly indebted to her for much of the information which has appeared in this chapter.

In her summary Joyce Bellamy suggests that the failure of Earle's involved problems of management, finance, labour and location. While the partnership appeared to have been prosperous throughout its currency it seems likely that the brothers made insufficient provision for depreciation and if death had not intervened they might themselves have had to face quite a serious financial situation within a few years. They had advantages, which their successors could not claim, namely a very good grounding in local business and numerous local contracts. Nevertheless if they had continued further capital would have had to have been introduced.

The public limited company inherited this situation—a chronic shortage of working capital. Over and over again this prevented the company from accepting orders which required finance over long periods and resulted in a dependence on bankers and creditors for running the concern because the subscribed capital was absorbed in land, buildings and stock.

Over the years the company was thus forced to pay out large sums in interest on money borrowed and was constantly approaching bankers for better terms. Indeed, they changed their bank four times in a period of 15 years. Again it seems unlikely that they made adequate allowance for depreciation and too often dividends were allowed to take precedence over reserves for depreciation.

Like most companies of its time it was basically product orientated; the quality of work produced was high but too often badly costed so that losses occurred. There is also some evidence that successive managers of the company failed to be very thrusting against competition. Cost-wise Earle's—and other local shipbuilders—were always at a disadvantage when compared with the yards on the Clyde, Tyne and Tees, particularly because coal and iron supplies were more expensive when conveyed to Hull.

Joyce Bellamy says:

'The history of the Company to 1900 provides several examples of over-optimism on the part of the management in accepting, at boom periods, large numbers of contracts for which the existing labour supply was insufficient. This was especially apparent in the early 1880s when local competition for labour developed and the men were enticed away from Earle's by higher wages. Furthermore, some of the directors and most of the shareholders were not experienced in the ship-building business—a factor which should not be ignored in the overall management of the concern at certain periods of its history. The financial instability of the Company became apparent when labour difficulties increased the cost of contracts and the final collapse in 1900 was due to severe losses on government contracts and additional costs arising from prolonged labour disputes for which the company had insufficient financial resources. Some of the difficulties which beset the public limited company were . . . due to a lack of foresight on the part of the management in over-contracting and paying high dividends at certain times, which induced the men to ask for higher wages and resulted in financial impoverishment.'

At that time, of course, there was no requirement that a private limited company should publish its accounts and thus its precise situation under the Wilson family is unknown, but presumably until 1918 it was profitable. There is no reason to believe that management was really ineffective at this time; it was just not efficient enough to survive the depression years of the early 1930s—but that, after all, was a very common experience of those days.

The day that rocked British Industry

Rolls Royce 1884-1971

O N 4 February 1971 Britain's most famous company declared itself bankrupt. British industry was shaken to its foundations. As one City broker said that grey afternoon, 'Life will never be the same again,' and with a fine sense of history, 'It must be rather like the day Queen Victoria died.'

The Times, ever portentous, pronounced the event to be 'much the most important company failure since before the war'. Harold Wilson's wife Mary was 'in a state of shock' and she felt 'as if we had lost the Rock of Gibraltar'.

Was British industry tarnished for ever? Would the Stock Market emulate its 1929 performance? 'The whole nation,' said one politician speaking at Derby, home of the doomed company, 'is shaken to its very foundations.'

Had the failure to develop one engine, the RB 211, really brought Britain's most famous company to its knees? People mourned not just an institution but that most valuable of assets —a reputation. We might have relinquished our Empire but at any rate we still had ROLLS-ROYCE.

For the beginnings of this once great concern we have to go back to Henry Royce and the closing years of the last century or, more specifically, to the year 1904 when he proudly drove his first car, with a two-cylinder 10 hp engine, 16 miles from his works in Manchester to his home at Knutsford in Cheshire.

Royce was the classic self-made man, the poor boy who fought his way to fame and riches. The son of an unsuccessful miller who died when Henry was nine, he had become a newspaper boy with only a year's schooling behind him. Later, when he was 14, through the generosity of an aunt he was apprenticed to the Great Northern Railway Works at Peterborough. But he had only been at Peterborough for three years when his aunt ran short of money and his apprenticeship was ended. From Peterborough he set out on a long weary search for work and eventually landed a job in an armaments factory in Leeds where he worked a 54 hour week for 11s. Here he was given his first introduction to electricity, at that time very much a pioneer science. The London Electric Light and Power Company was one of the first in the field and they advertised for a 'tester'. Royce applied and got the job. At the early age of 19 he was Chief Electrical Engineer in charge of the scheme for the electric lighting of the streets of Liverpool. Royce learned fast and started to enjoy himself but the company went out of business and again he was unemployed.

By now Royce was determined to start his own business. He had saved £20 and had a friend, A. E. Claremont, with £50. In 1884 they joined together to form F. H. Royce & Company of Cook Street, Manchester, with the object of trading as electrical engineers. So the whole Rolls-Royce empire was founded on a precarious capital of £70 which, even in the light of the events of 1971, is not so bad.

At first the company specialised in electric light filaments, bulbs and electric bell sets. Royce was not an inventor but an improver. At that time the existing dynamos were unreliable and erratic. Royce set about improving their performance and companies began to buy the Royce dynamos for lighting factories and ships.

Slowly but surely the company progressed and in 1894

changed its name to Royce Ltd, 'Electrical and Mechanical
Engineers and Manufacturers of Dynamos, Motors and
Kindred articles'. This limited company took over from the
earlier partnership and had an early success with electric
cranes which filled a place in the market between the steam
crane, which was anything but a precision piece of plant and
which took a long time to get going, and hand pullies and
slings. By October 1897 they had orders worth £6,000 and less
than two years later this figure had risen to £20,000. To meet
the demand the company's capital was increased from the
original very modest £70 to £30,000. Then, just as Royce
and his colleagues were all set for a great leap forward the
demand for their cranes began to fall off. They were good,
they were very good, but they were also expensive and already
Royce had adopted the precept that people remember the
quality long after the price has been forgotten. But in this
case it didn't work out. Electric cranes had caught on and
were being imported from America, Belgium and Germany
and all of them undercut Royce on price. Royce refused to
lower his standards; soon his order books were empty, his
labour force only half occupied and Royce himself had the
problem of servicing his new increase in capital. Only then
did he turn to cars and even that may have been an accident.
In 1903, in spite of the crane setback, he had a reasonably
good year from the sales of his dynamo and he bought a car,
a 10 h.p. French model. The story goes that he became so
impatient with this car's faults and bad design that in exas-
peration he decided to produce his own model. Certainly
there is evidence that his car was noisy and vibrated badly;
the engine raced when stationary.

During the winter of 1903-4 he worked very hard, assisted
by some young mechanics, to produce a car which would
overcome these and the other faults he had noted. Royce,
lacking education, was unable to invent except by practical
experiment and so, as he devised each component, he tested it.
In his quest for perfection he made some of the first simulators;
one was a 'bumping machine' which would concentrate several

thousands of miles of running over the poor roads of that time into a few hours.

Royce was a hard taskmaster both on himself and his men. Stories about his phenomenal energy, coupled with a fantastic attention to detail, are legion. For months on end he would hardly go to bed, simply catnapping at his bench. Apprentices were told to take him bread and milk because otherwise he would not have eaten at all.

His attitude to his employees would have made the modern trade unionist die of apoplexy. Many of his assistants worked up to 100 hours a week, for which they received five shillings. He frequently demanded that they worked far into the evenings and over the weekends. Yet most of his colleagues and subordinates enjoyed working for him and his enormous mechanical skill and his high standards were admired. In spite of the intolerable conditions which he imposed on his men there was no shortage of keen mechanics eager to learn from the great Royce.

When Royce's car first appeared there was nothing very new about it in details; the startling feature was the tremendous improvement in overall reliability and comfort which it presented. The battery and ignition system had several improvements based on Royce's electrical experience. The engine had two cylinders and the rear wheels were driven through a cone clutch and three speed gearbox. The maximum speed was in the region of 30 mph and the car weighed about 15 cwt. To driver, passenger and pedestrian alike the most outstanding feature was its silent operation, a Rolls-Royce tradition from the very beginning, enshrined in a much more recent advertisement which said that at 100 mph the loudest sound in a Rolls-Royce was the ticking of the electric clock. And soon afterwards Rolls-Royce proudly announced that they had eliminated even this noise.

Royce made three of his 10 hp cars, all of which have been lost to posterity. One he used himself; the other was given to his original partner, Claremont, and the third went to Mr Henry Edmunds who was at that time well-known in motoring

E

circles and had recently joined the Board of Royce's. This gift had far reaching repercussions for one of Henry Edmunds's friends was none other than the Honourable Charles Rolls.

Soon a most fruitful co-operation was to begin, but on the face of it the chances of success were slim. The difference between the two men could not have been greater. Charles Rolls, the third son of Lord Llangattock, had enjoyed a comfortable childhood at his family's country seat in Monmouthshire. He went to Eton where he was somewhat ridiculed for his early interest in electricity and engineering. At Cambridge he was the first undergraduate to have a car. He took a mechanical engineering degree and soon became a well-known motor enthusiast, frequently competing in races. In 1900 he won the Thousand Mile Reliability Trial, driving a 12 hp Panhard, and three years later he broke a world speed record by doing 93 mph in a 70 hp Moors.

In 1902 he started his own business, C. S. Rolls & Co. for the sale and repair of cars. As such he was always on the lookout for reliable makes of car to sell and his business prospered sufficiently to invite Claude Johnson to join him as a partner in 1904.

At their first meeting, arranged by Edmunds, Rolls and Royce got on very well and, on the spot, they made an agreement. Their two businesses were to continue independently but Rolls undertook to market Royce's cars under the joint name Rolls-Royce. The arrangement was particularly exciting to Royce because although he was perhaps the foremost engineer of his day he had very little marketing experience and no distributive organisation.

Royce undertook to make and Rolls to sell, four models, ranging from the 10 hp two cylinder to a 30 hp six cylinder at prices from £395 to £890 for the chassis only.

The 10's made a notable impression at the 1904 Paris Show and won a gold medal. *Motor News* said cautiously: 'I am rarely tempted into the realms of prophecy but I venture the opinion that Messrs Royce and company will make a high reputation for themselves with all their British cars.'

Given the excellence of the car, Rolls was able to put Royce's vehicles on the map with just the right people. In fact, Rolls was an exceedingly clever public relations man with excellent connections. He arranged, for example, to meet HRH the Duke of Connaught, one of Queen Victoria's sons, at Folkestone in a 10 hp Rolls-Royce; when the Headmaster of Eton retired Rolls made sure that the Old Etonians gave him a Rolls-Royce. And at the army manoeuvres in 1905 there was Rolls with his car again, driving the staff generals. Rolls's partner, Claude Johnson was also an inspired publicist who put abroad the gospel of Rolls-Royce superiority. One of the ways he did this was to race the cars at every opportunity. In 1906 the London/Monte Carlo record time was beaten by Rolls who cut just 1½ minutes off the previous record. Two of the 20 hp models were entered in the 1905 Isle of Man Tourist Trophy and in this race a Rolls-Royce took second place.

The famous Silver Ghost appeared at the very end of 1906 and had an unbroken run until 1925. During this period nearly 6,500 Silver Ghosts were produced and set the seal on the marque's success.

Before the Silver Ghost appeared Rolls and Royce had decided to cement their informal partnership and on 16 March 1906 Rolls-Royce Ltd was registered with a capital of £60,000, £10,00 of which was contributed by Rolls. C. S. Rolls & Company disappeared completely in the merger and Rolls no longer sold cars of any other make. The electrical side of Royce's Manchester business continued to operate under the name of Royce until after his death but all motor car production was placed in the hands of the new company. The first directors of Rolls-Royce were Royce, Rolls, Johnson and a man called Briggs who had encouraged the merger. Immediately the new company began to look for production premises and settled on Derby where a site of over 12 acres was purchased. The new factory was opened in July 1908.

This ambitious move required a considerable increase in share capital and at the end of 1908 the company went 'public' and £100,000 of shares were offered with the stipulation that unless £50,000 was provided within a given period the flotation would be abandoned. Rolls-Royce cars had already made an impression but not, it appeared, sufficient for the British public to risk their money and as the closing date approached only £41,000 had been subscribed. The situation was saved by Briggs who provided £10,000.

The prospectus issued at the time of the flotation stated the directors' salaries. Royce was named Chief Engineer and Works Director at £1,250 per annum and 4% of the profits in excess of £10,000. Rolls was Technical Managing Director at £750 per annum and 4% of the surplus profits; and Claremont, Royce's original partner was named Chairman and Commercial Adviser at £250 and 2% of the surplus profits. From this it would seem that somehow Claremont had lost a lot of ground because, after all, he was Royce's first backer.

In 1908 it was agreed by the Board that all the resources of the company should be concentrated on the Silver Ghost which, in the period before the first world war, won prize after prize. By that time there was a considerable export market for this excellent car, including the United States. But the most enthusiastic export buyers were the Maharajahs of India. For example, the Maharajah of Mysore acquired eight Rolls-Royces and the tradition has continued up to recent times—in 1962 the Maharajah of Patiala owned 23 and the Nizam of Hyderabad no less than 50. By the outbreak of the first world war the company had representatives and repair organisations not only in the United States and India but also in France, Spain, Austria, Canada and Australia. Just before the outbreak of war the Czar of Russia bought two Silver Ghosts from the Paris showrooms.

By 1914 Rolls-Royce Ltd was securely established as the manufacturers of the best car in the world. Royce's technical expertise had been married to Rolls' genius for organisation and Johnson's immense talent for advertising and publicity. But Rolls was no more. A chance meeting with Wilbur Wright in 1907 had turned him from motoring to flying and in April 1910 he resigned as managing director of the company and less than three months later his plane crashed during a competition at Bournemouth and he was killed instantly. The remains of his plane were towed away by a Silver Ghost.

Inevitably a number of Rolls found their way to France at the outbreak of war. After all it had been promoted as a quality car for top people and the top people took their own cars with them. For the first two years of the war a team of four Rolls-Royces was responsible for the King's messenger services between the British General Headquarters and the French ports. In the two years of their service not one of these cars ever broke down.

Rolls-Royce began making armoured cars and by March 1915 there were 78 of these on active service. All production was devoted to the war effort and there were no cars available for private customers. Although the plating increased the weight of the car by three tons the only necessary alteration to the chassis was the fitting of extra leaf springs back and front. The engine remained unchanged and under favourable conditions could still reach a speed of 70 mph. Rolls-Royce armoured car squadrons were organised and saw service in France, Africa and the Middle East. Even the camel-riding T. E. Lawrence became a devotee, stating that 'all the Turks in Arabia could not fight a single Rolls-Royce'. Indeed on one occasion he blew up two bridges, destroyed a length of railway line, captured two Turkish posts and caused havoc to a Turkish cavalry regiment in a single day with only three Rolls-Royces. 'A Rolls in the desert was above rubies,' Lawrence reported enthusiastically.

But armoured cars were not Rolls-Royce's only contribution to the war effort. In 1914 the Government ordered the company to produce aero-engines of French design but Royce considered them shoddy and immediately set about producing his own plans for a superior engine. The engine which finally emerged, the brainchild of a man who was already sick from overwork and malnutrition, was the 200 hp Eagle. It powered a number of the early fighters and also the Handley-Page 0400 twin engined bomber, the Fairey seaplane and the Vickers Vimy bomber. By the end of the war the capacity of this engine had been stretched to 360 hp and Rolls-Royce were working on a new 600 hp engine—the Condor—which was intended to be used in the Handley-Page V/1500 bomber. Rolls-Royce also produced the 75 hp Hawk and the Falcon for the Bristol Fighter. Altogether Rolls-Royce provided nearly 70% of the aero-engines used in British aircraft in the first world war, the majority being Eagles, of which they supplied some 4,000.

At the end of the war Rolls-Royce adjusted themselves to the needs of peace. The first new car was the Twenty which was launched in 1922 and was designed to appeal to the growing number of owner-drivers. It was a smaller car, of course, than the Silver Ghost but manufactured to the same exacting standards. The Silver Ghost ceased production in 1925 and the following year Royce lost another faithful colleague in Johnson, who as Joint Managing Director had been in the company from the very beginning. Johnson built the legend and formed the distinctive Rolls-Royce personality.

The company was now in a curious position because Royce's health had broken down in 1911 and thereafter he seldom if ever appeared at Derby and worked on the Riviera at his home 'Le Canadel', maintaining a nucleus of designers there and keeping continual contact with headquarters by long memoranda. Nevertheless in 1926 the company's situation was extremely satisfactory. In 1905 the capital of Royce's at Manchester was about £100,000. In 1926 capital employed amounted to £814,000 and profits had risen from £5,390 in 1905 to £164,000 in 1926, a whacking great 20% of capital employed.

Following the Silver Ghost was the Phantom I, a majestic vehicle equipped with 100 hp engine and a maximum speed of 80 mph. In 1929 Phantom I was replaced by Phantom II and Phantom III was the first car to appear (in 1936) without the blessing of Royce, who died in 1934. Meanwhile, in 1931 Rolls-Royce had bought up the famous Bentley Marque and the $3\frac{1}{2}$ litre Rolls-Bentley appeared which was replaced in 1936 by the $4\frac{1}{2}$ litre, a car which made a tremendous impact in sports car and racing circles. Bentley's were a victim of the depression and Rolls-Royce had their difficulties too. The American factory, which had been founded in 1919 and was in the hands of a subsidiary company, was declared bankrupt in 1934.

At this time of depression it was perhaps a good thing for the company that they had begun to develop aero-engines in the first world war. Afterwards they did not throw away the experience they had gained and in the 20's and 30's ever-increasing number of planes were powered by Rolls-Royce engines. The Kestrel, developed in the late 20's, was a revolutionary new engine. It used special aluminium alloys developed by the company and was responsible for many British air triumphs. The direct successor of the Kestrel was the Merlin engine which powered the Spitfires and Hurricanes in the Battle of Britain. The Kestrel and Merlin were developed by Rolls-Royce with their own finance and at their own risk, but as the war clouds gathered again the government financed a number of Rolls-Royce factories all over the country which were, however, entirely under the company's technical control. They also financed a substantial enlargement of the Derby works. In 1943 Rolls-Royce factories were turning out 18,000 Merlins a year and on the ground Rolls-Royce was no less vital : many tanks were powered with their engines.

Jet engines, eventually to be the company's undoing, occupied much of the company's technological resources during the early part of the war and the first Rolls-Royce jet flew in 1943. From that time onwards the old divisions—motor cars, diesels, gas turbines, oil engines became less and less important financially. Aero-engines established Rolls-Royce as a premier company—and perhaps was the prime cause of their eventual bankruptcy. At the time of the disaster

capital employed had increased to £223 million and employees
had reached an all time high of nearly 90,000.

From the very start, in the war years and afterwards, Rolls
were involved in some of the most important jet contracts.
They pioneered vertical take-off, the first turbo-jet in airline
service, the first turbo-fan in airline service, the first jet air-
liner to undertake a regular transatlantic run. By the mid-
sixties Rolls-Royce was able to claim that half the civil aircraft
sold in the West with turbine engines since the war had been
powered by them. Their engines were in the Canberra, the
Saab Lensen, the Hawker Hunter, the Vickers Valiant, the
Vickers Viscount, the Convair 600, the Douglas DC8, the
Boeing 707, the Vickers VC10 the BAC one-eleven—just to
mention a few of the 50-odd major post-war engine contracts.

Were they killed by their reputation? During the last 20
years the development of aero-engines have put increasing
technological and economic demands on the companies engaged in this work. By September 1971 the total cost of
launching the RB 211 had risen from an estimated £65.5
million in 1968 to £225 million. The challenge grew greater
and greater but in the Rolls-Royce tradition it was unthink-
able that they should step down at any point. Was it technical
arrogance that killed Rolls-Royce, the arrogance of the proud
engineers who overwhelmingly ruled the company? Did they
feel they had to succeed at any cost? Did they take on too
much?

Rolls-Royce never stinted in anything they did. In 1970
they revealed that while the government had invested £33.6
million in the launching of the Dart, Avon, Conway and
Spey engines, Rolls-Royce had contributed an enormous £90
million of its own funds, very largely speculative. Admittedly
the gamble came off on that occasion because total business
from these engines was estimated at £1,260 million. But with
the RB 211 it looks as if Rolls-Royce's traditions ensnared
them. They gambled too high and lost. Perhaps they were
arrogant, perhaps they had no alternative. Sir Denning Pearson their ex-chairman summed up their situation after the

crash : 'Building a new engine would not guarantee we stayed in business. Not building one would certainly guarantee that we went out of business.'

Not only had the engine to be developed successfully but Rolls-Royce had to sell it. Here they had to meet competition, principally from the States, of an intensity they had never known before. By the late sixties Rolls-Royce were, rightly, obsessed with the American market. This obsession made the temptation of underpricing very considerable. In the late sixties a price-cutting war developed. In 1967 devaluation led Rolls to cut their price for the RB 211 by 5%. Their principal rivals were General Electric and Pratt & Whitney. Early in 1968 General Electric cut their price; Rolls countered by lowering theirs still further. At the same time the Americans were unhappy about their balance of payments; the American airlines could not disregard the needs of their own economy. It was said that to buy the RB 211 would be a stigma, un-American.

Nevertheless, backed by a government assurance that support would be forthcoming if they gained a suitable contract Rolls-Royce continued the most determined sales drive they had ever made in America. They were after the business of Lockheed and McDonnel Douglas, both of which were developing their own air buses. In an all-out effort the company spent £80,000 on transatlantic air fares and a further £6,000 on telephone calls. It has been estimated that the company's marketing activities on this project was over £400,000.

The final deal, as announced in Britain, was that two American airlines and Air Holdings, a British company, had ordered a total of 144 of the Lockheed L1011 Air Bus, each of which would be powered with three Rolls-Royce engines. Rolls-Royce was to receive £150 million from these initial orders with a possible £1,000 million from future sales.

In fact, with the benefit of hindsight, it appears that this contract, which was hailed in Britain as the greatest sales achievement since the war, killed off Rolls-Royce. There was no provision for the effects of inflation; there were savage

penalty clauses which gave Lockheed huge sums in the event
of late delivery; and the time limits were exceptionally short.
The whole contract had to be completed by November 1971.

To make matters worse Rolls-Royce had wildly mis-
calculated development costs. At first they estimated them to
be £65.5 million, of which the government offered £47.1
million. Almost at once the error in their calculations became
apparent and the share price started to drift downwards.
Rolls-Royce's reserves were just not enough to pay for the
RB 211's development.

Even when the Spey had been in process of development
it had proved impossible to provide the funds required from
the profit and loss account. These funds were therefore treated
as capital expenditure and the development costs were
covered from the orders as placed. This was a risky manoeuvre
but on that occasion the orders had covered the gamble.
However, with the costs so much higher for the RB 211 Rolls-
Royce capitalised launching costs not just to the extent of
existing orders, but according to their estimates of what future
orders might be.

The fate of Rolls-Royce was sealed when they ran into
considerable technical problems, which delayed the RB 211's
production and the penalty clauses loomed large. The RB 211
was the largest jet engine ever to be manufactured and Rolls-
Royce found that it demanded entirely new testing facilities;
they spent several million pounds designing and producing
apparatus to test the engine in high cross-winds and this was
only a single aspect of the test requirements. There was a
further factor : continual wage demands, strikes, and rising
costs accounted for about 15% of the RB 211's increased
expense which by 1970 was more than double the original
estimate.

Rolls-Royce made their own internal economies but they
were not, and could not be, enough. Late in 1970 it was clear
that only two things could save Rolls-Royce. They must either
renegotiate the contract with Lockheed or the government
must advance further massive loans.

Lockheed were sympathetic but unmoved. They had themselves suffered a huge loss on an American government contract. But at first it looked as though the British government would come to Rolls-Royce's aid. In November 1970, having been informed that the development costs of the RB 211 had by then risen to £135 million it advanced another £42 million and arranged for bank loans to the value of £18 million. However, these advances were conditional on an accountant's examination of Rolls-Royce's financial situation. Inevitably this report took time to prepare and it looked as though Rolls-Royce had made their approaches too late: by now they were even short of cash to pay salaries and wages.

When the accountants reported it seemed as if Rolls-Royce had again made a mistake. In the accountant's view the £135 million estimate was short of the mark and it looked as though the RB 211 would absorb something like £220 million before it could go into production. This meant that even if no penalty clauses for late delivery were invoked Rolls-Royce would lose a cool £110,000 on each engine or £60 million on the whole contract. If penalty clauses were invoked, which now seemed certain, they would lose a further £50 million. On 4 February 1971 Mr Corfield, Minister of Aviation, told the Commons that the nation would have to pay out a further £150 million to save Rolls-Royce.

At this point the government was in an unenviable dilemma. With an economy far from stable £150 million was an enormous amount to pay out, but Rolls-Royce still enshrined some of the world's most advanced technological expertise, employed a labour force of nearly 90,000 and probably kept almost as many in employment with sub-contractors. If Rolls-Royce was allowed to go out of business scores of other lesser companies might be ruined as well. In the event they chose to allow Rolls-Royce to go bankrupt, thus cancelling the obligation to Lockheed, and then to reactivate Rolls-Royce by nationalisation. The nationalised company was, of course, minus the contract and comprised only aero-engine, marine and industrial gas turbine divisions of Rolls-Royce. The other divisions, it was decided should be sold off privately.

Thus it was that on 4 February 1971 Rolls-Royce declared itself bankrupt and 19 days later, on 23 February, the new nationalised company Rolls-Royce (1971) Ltd was registered.

Almost a year later, in January 1972, the government issued a White Paper which answered, or attempted to answer, criticisms which were made at the time of the bankruptcy. This White Paper was in effect a reply to a series of articles which appeared in *The Times* at the time of the collapse. Then *The Times* made two assertions. The first was that the Rolls' accepting house syndicate, led by Lazards, was under the impression that the government entered into an unconditional commitment in November 1970 to provide Rolls-Royce with an additional £42 million of launching aid. This assertion was based on Heads of Agreement, dated 9 November 1970, which set out the conditions under which the government, the Bank of England, Lloyds and the Midland Bank would together put up a total of a further £60 million.

But this 'secret' agreement, to which *The Times* apparently had access, did not contain any prior conditions about a satisfactory report from the accountant although in the 'official' story circulating at the time, and as indicated earlier in this narrative, there was such a condition. *The Times* contended that Cooper Brothers were asked, on 24 November 1970, to prepare a report on Rolls-Royce's profits and cash forecasts up to 1974 but this was not complete by February 1971 when the company was put into the hands of the receiver.

On this point the White Paper stated:

'The Accepting Houses were not informed by the Bank of England that the sum of £42 million to be provided by the government would be subject to check by the independent accountant because this check was essentially a matter of determining the exact sum to be paid by the government to Rolls-Royce and the Bank of England took the view that it was not a matter of such significance as to require them to draw it specifically to the attention of the Accepting Houses.'

The Times points out that without the government's extra
£42 million commitment in November 1970 the Accepting
houses might have announced their refusal to continue their
£20 million acceptance facility when it came up for renewal
in April 1971, thus causing a crisis of confidence. Rolls-Royce's
trade creditors might have started demanding cash payments,
or least have reduced credit terms, thus giving the company's
cash position a major blow.

It was to meet these dangers that the Rolls-Royce Board
put out a press release and arranged for a letter to go to their
major suppliers on 11 November 1970, on which day Sir
Denning Pearson resigned as chairman, to be replaced by
Lord Cole.

In this press release it was said:

'Cash requirements have been under discussion with the
government, with the Governor of the Bank of England, with
the company's bankers and the accepting houses. As a result
of these discussions the government has undertaken to provide
substantial additional launching aid in respect of the RB
211-22 engine and satisfactory arrangements have been made
with the banks to meet the company's needs.'

There was no mention of any strings attached to this support, nor was there any indication of any such requirements in
the letter which the directors of the company sent out to their
principal trade creditors, also in November 1970.

As a consequence many creditor companies felt they were
seriously misled by these events and *The Times* cites Tube
Investments who, in April 1971, indicated in their annual
accounts that the company thought it prudent to make provision for a £2.1 million loss as a consequence of the Rolls-
Royce failure. In his statement the chairman, Lord Plowden,
stated, 'We accept that it was for us to gauge the risks involved in continuing to trade with Rolls-Royce and that the

responsibility for the losses incurred therefore rests with us. Our attitude was, however, materially influenced by a letter dated November 11 1970 from Rolls-Royce to Reynolds Tube as a major supplier, which stated that the financial difficulty had been discussed with the Government and private sources, and overcome with their further support. There was no reference to any conditions attaching to that support.'

Since then the position of the unsecured creditors has, perhaps, improved. At first it was thought that there would be virtually nothing at all to offer them; but by March of 1971 there was talk of 12½p in the £ and by June the receiver felt that he could announce that unsecured creditors should get 50p; by October he considered they would get repayment in full and that there might be even a little left over for the ordinary shareholders.

This was an extraordinary, if heartening position. It can only have come about because as negotiations proceeded the government decided, or was forced to realise, that the company's assets were far more valuable than they had at first thought. *The Times* goes further and suggests that the government had accepted a certain moral obligation to deal generously with the receiver in the interests of those unsecured creditors who might have been misled by the November 1970 episode.

The second assertion which *The Times* made in February 1971 was that in their opinion the government was incorrect in stating that they had no option but to allow Rolls-Royce to go into receivership. Good City legal opinion, they said, considered that alternative courses were open.

The comments of *The Times* on this situation in January 1972 are interesting :

'In late January (1971) Rolls-Royce received a new technical and financial assessment of the RB 211. The Board had taken legal advice, which led them to the conclusion in the light of the latest evidence that they were at risk under Section 332 of the Companies Act; that is that they might be a party to a company continuing to trade when there was no reasonable prospect of its creditors being paid.'

The government took the view that, although the Act is not binding on the Crown, they could not be party to a contravention of that section. Few would contest that decision.

'But the burden of proof of active intent to defraud creditors under the Section is heavy. For a considerable period before February 1971 the creditors of Rolls-Royce would have had little prospect of repayment in the event that the Government ceased to back the project.

'It would have been difficult to argue convincingly that the Government were party to fraudulent trading, if they had allowed Rolls-Royce to draw on the £42 million promised the previous November (while they attempted to renegotiate the RB 211 contract). Or indeed if they had decided to nationalise the company outright.

'This is quite different from the issue of whether Rolls-Royce in the hands of a receiver strengthened the Government's bargaining hand with Lockheed and the Nixon administration.'

And *The Times* concludes:

'For the fact is that in that period of crisis at the end of January, the Government were determined to kill the RB 211 programme.'

What is the situation today? Although perhaps not as grim as originally envisaged it is still grim enough. The future of a British aerospace industry remains unresolved and there are still creditors of Rolls-Royce to the tune of some £130 million. Maybe they will be paid in full in due course but many of them are increasingly anxious for the money to start coming in.

The trouble here is that a political consideration may be important. In February 1972 *The Times* asked:

'Do the Government wish creditors to be repaid in full and shareholders—the key here being worker shareholders—to recover at least something from their ruinous investment? Or do they wish to emphasize the harshness of business failure and strengthen the arguments that Rolls-Royce was beyond rescue?'

Let *The Times* have the last word. Certainly, at the time of writing, there is no sign of even a first dividend for the creditors.

A Founder Member of the British Motor Car Industry

The Lanchester Engine Co. Ltd. 1896-1904

FOR ALL—and they are a rapidly growing band—of those who revere vintage and veteran cars the name Lanchester is held in great respect. But most of these early examples of British engineering ingenuity are the products of The Lanchester Motor Company. Much rarer is the Lanchester produced by The Lanchester Engine Company Ltd, which was awarded a gold medal in 1899 at the Richmond Exhibition and Trials and is now preserved in the Science Museum, London. Much revered, too, in the annals of technology is the founder of that company, F. W. Lanchester. Unfortunately his brilliant technical ability was unmatched by any similar business acumen and while, as the years went by, his name became increasingly famous with the motoring fraternity he enjoyed little or none of The Lanchester Motor Company's success.

In the 1890s the motorcar industry was barely established in Britain. France had already built up a considerable export trade but in Britain there were only three companies concerned with the manufacture of motorcars—the Daimler Motor Company, established in 1896, the Lanchester Engine

F

Company, and the Motor Manufacturing Company. This last concern was the creation of Harry J. Lawson who has been described as a 'flamboyant company promoter and syndicate floater, who was prominent if not notorious in his efforts to finance the early motor car industry'. His first venture, Lawson's Great Horseless Carriage Company had come to nothing but he had also launched the Daimler Motor Company. By the end of the century Daimler, relieved of Lawson's rather erratic interest, was already producing cars with a considerable name for their performance and quality. A Daimler had been driven successfully from John O'Groats to Land's End and already royalty were beginning to choose Daimler as *the* car.

Lanchester was a lad who grew up on the crest of the scientific and engineering wave so vividly described by H. G. Wells in many of his books. He went to the Normal School of Science at South Kensington where he showed a strong sense of individuality by devising his own reading programme because it did not contain the subjects he wanted. Thus he left the college without qualifying.

His career was soon centred on Birmingham which, as P. W. Kingsford has said in his most informative study of Lanchester contained in 'Business History', was in the 90s 'poised between the town of a thousand workshops and the home of the great industries of the 20th century'. He became assistant manager of the Forward Gas Engine Company and, soon afterwards, works manager. It was here he made his discovery famous in aerodynamics, the Vortex theory of sustention. At much the same time he started to build what the Birmingham historian, A. Briggs, has described as 'the first full-sized British petrol-driven motor-car'.

His three experimental cars, built between 1894 and 1899 without doubt established him as one of the great pioneers of the motor car and it is one of these that is preserved to this day in the Science Museum. They were a product of enormous mental and physical energy, coupled with an extraordinary ingenuity for overcoming problems by numerous inventions.

Many parts he devised are permanent features of the automobile today.

In theory at any rate Lanchester had a lively appreciation of the money to be made from this new industry and the interest which his experimental cars aroused decided him to push forward to production. While he was at the Forward Gas Engine Company he had an experimental workshop of his own, housed in an iron shed at Ladywood Road. Now he moved to the Armourer Mills in the Sparkbrook district, into premises which had been a rolling mill and tube-boring factory.

The first three experimental cars had been financed to the tune of about £4,000 by a syndicate in which Lanchester and James and Allan Whitfield contributed one third each. This was the genesis of The Lanchester Engine Company and in 1899 it was agreed among the three that they should find more money to go into production.

Lanchester's obvious technological genius attracted the Pugh brothers and J. S. Taylor, men who had already collaborated in the establishments of the Whitworth Cycle Company and later the Rudge Whitworth Company of Coventry. They had no experience of motorcar manufacture but at that date very few had—and they had already achieved considerable success in the cycle industry.

At the end of November 1899 a new agreement was made in which the ex-Whitworth people bought a quarter of the first syndicate's assets for £4,000, of which £2,000 went to Lanchester and £1,000 each to the Whitfields. These assets included a staggering 20 British patents and nine foreign patents already taken out by Lanchester.

The second syndicate then formally became the Lanchester Engine Company Ltd in December 1899. The new company's authorised capital was £100,000, of which £42,525 was paid up. However of this sum only £25,000 was subscribed in cash. The two Pughs, J. S. Taylor, James Whitfield, and a man named Hamilton Barnsley, were the directors of the new company. Lanchester declined the invitation to become

Managing Director partly because he considered the cash resources too small but also because he did not want financial responsibility.

Since he made this quite clear in a memorandum it is perhaps surprising that he was appointed General Manager because while in this position he would have no legal financial responsibilities it was evident that in practice he could influence day-to-day financial management very considerably. Under his agreement with the company he was appointed at a salary of £350 per annum which was to rise to £450 after two years. In the early days particularly his influence was very considerable. He was not only General Manager but also Works Manager, at any rate for the first year, as well as Designer—since he was the man who knew all the technical answers to the problems of the new product the company was to launch. Technically, his assistants and workers were good. One of Lanchester's brothers looked after sales and publicity and was also Company Secretary and another was Chief Technical Assistant. The men on the shop floor were well chosen; eager, enthusiastic craftsmen with confidence and pride in the new venture. Lanchester was both respected as a man and revered as a genius.

The first model planned for the company was the Lanchester 10 and Lanchester himself busily planned the organisation and the layout of the works to cope with production. He selected and installed the plant and designed and made the jigs, special tools, patterns and gauges required.

Production did not begin until 1901 and for two years money was spent without hope of immediate return. However, the first car went on the road in August of that year and six or seven had been made by December. In the annual report of the company for the year ending July 1902 the directors said 'some of our cars in the hands of the public have been running upwards of a year and proving in every way satisfactory'. In January 1903 at the Earls Court Stanley Automobile Exhibition—the forerunner of the present Motor

Show—the company displayed 12 of the 10 hp cars with different types of bodywork and finish.

It was in this same year that *The Times* correspondent wrote lyrically 'for grace combined with efficiency it is difficult to better the Lanchester. We have here something of the beauty of the carriage of old combined with the power and speed of a new concept of vehicle.'

Originality of design and technical success singled out Lanchester's cars for special mention. In particular the Lanchester brought to the car of its day new standards in reliability, silence and comfort. The absence of vibration was achieved by balancing wheels and cantilever springing and incorporated such novel features as a pre-selector mechanism on the epicyclic gear. The Lanchester was never intended to be the car for the masses—not that they had been initiated into the joys of motoring at this early stage in any case—but it found great favour with what was then the upper end of the motoring market so that in the first four years sales averaged 100 a year, which for those days was very good indeed. In fact the directors of The Lanchester Engine Company could be excused for thinking that all was set for a long period of prosperity.

On the technical side the problems which Lanchester overcame were enormous. At that time there was no buying-in of ready-made components as is the practice in the motor industry of today. Lanchester's organisation was very far from being an assembly shop and practically everything in his cars, except the rims, lamps and tyres, was made in the works. Lanchester was a perfectionist and, uncontrolled by his directors, spent as much time as he wished in solving the various problems which presented themselves with all the ingenuity and patience at his command.

For example, when production began nuts and bolts with Whitworth threads were used but it was found that vibration soon led to them slackening off. Thus Lanchester devised his own range of standard threads and worked out the exact torques necessary to prevent over-stressing or slackening.

At that date satisfactory ball bearings did not exist either, and so he made and fitted roller bearings of his own design. For this and other precision work he introduced what is now known as the centreless grinder. His splined shaft, which was included in the Lanchester 10 from an early date, was later universally used in cars of all makes. Again he was not satisfied with the oils available and this led him to design a blending and filtering plant to provide oil for his cars.

He was also a visionary who saw the possibilities of mass production based on standardisation and the interchangeability of parts which, in turn, demanded considerable accuracy. This technique had never been undertaken before for a machine of such complexity as the motorcar and the close tolerances which he laid down cost considerable sums of money to maintain.

In some areas, however, Lanchester saved the company considerable sums of money. Originally he was instructed by the directors to obtain the bodywork from outside firms but this presented difficulties because the bodybuilders could or would not work to the precise instructions embodied in drawings, gauges and templates supplied by The Lanchester Engine Company. When the bodywork was delivered to the works it frequently had to be altered and thus production was held up. Lanchester's decision to manufacture himself saved a considerable amount of money because not only was the chassis and bodywork interchangeable but the necessity to carry high stocks was largely eliminated.

But in spite of high technical achievements and a very good reception for the Lanchester trouble was at hand. It was easy to be wise after the event but it is also possible to say, quite fairly, that the directors, as financiers, should have read the signals earlier and taken the necessary counter measures. If they had The Lanchester Engine Company could have had a long and prosperous life.

There were two reasons for the company's downfall: shortage of working capital and a development programme, instituted by a mechanical genius, which was entirely uncontrolled from the point of view of expense. As P. W. Kingsford has said in his monograph, it is very doubtful indeed if the initial provision of capital had any relation to planned expenditure at all. The directors, conversant with the bicycle industry, did not understand the investment required for motorcar manufacture, although it is only fair in making this stricture to remind ourselves that these were very early days for the car industry.

Many years afterwards, in the 30s, Lanchester wrote on the situation as it was in July of 1903. Between that date and 1899 the paid up capital had increased by only £15,070 to £57,595 plus a debenture issue of £25,000. In the year ending July 1903 there was a net profit of £8,669 on a turnover of approximately £80,000.

Liabilities to creditors amounted to about £20,000 and instead of increasing their own investment the directors decided to seek outside help to bring the capital up to the authorised total of £100,000. A prospectus was drawn up inviting subscription for a further 42,405 £1 shares but no support was forthcoming. So the company went bankrupt.

After it had been under a receiver for a year (during which time Lanchester remained as General Manager and there were very few material changes in organisation) the directors regained their confidence. The company was reconstructed as The Lanchester Motor Company in which the directors took up additional shares and the creditors accepted preference shares.

It was obviously decided that Lanchester should be the scapegoat and he ceased to be General Manager and became Technical Consultant at a fee of £250 per annum. He was also forced to surrender 2,000 of his shares and the value of the shares from the first company was reduced by half. A Managing Director was appointed and in the next five years profits averaging nearly £13,000 were recorded—and they increased steadily thereafter.

There are three main contributory factors for the failure of the original Lanchester company: Lanchester should never have been General Manager, his directors failed to take the close interest in the business which their positions demanded, and economic circumstances arising out of the South African war were sufficient to push a tottering company down a financial precipice.

Perhaps the most destructive element in the company's short history was the failure of communication between Lanchester the technologist and his directors as businessmen. It is an old, old story and Lanchester as an undoubted genius, was probably not the easiest of men to work with. It also seems likely, reading between the lines, that the directors, having ridden the crest of the cycle boom expected quick and easy returns on their money. Lanchester was always being pushed to make decisions against his technical judgment.

In 1902, without reference to Lanchester, the directors decided that a small car, a *Voiturette*, should be put on the market. Lanchester prepared a design at short notice against his better judgment and he was then told to go into production. Lanchester asked for £50,000 for production facilities. The directors could not fault his figures but were appalled at the investment required, so they shelved the project.

Then the directors were bitten by the small car bug and they undertook the agency for the sale in Birmingham and the Midlands of the Oldsmobile, at a discount of 10% for single cars, and 12½% for orders of six or more. This venture was, however, a failure.

Right at the beginning the seeds of dissension had been sown when the directors decided that the Lanchester 10 should sell at £450. Apparently they reached this figure from their own market research without any reference to production costs. Lanchester, who had done his homework, contended that the economic selling price should be £600. Eventually both sides agreed on £525 but this was merely a compromise without any apparent reference to the profit margins necessary to sustain the company.

If the directors, at this distance of time, seem to be unaware of what might be termed normal conditions of business, even if they were involved in a new industry, they were probably even less aware of the state of the economy around them. The outbreak of the South African war in 1899 meant that peace-time expansion slowed considerably and income tax and indirect taxes were both increased. Patriotism also demanded the diversion of investments into War Loans, Exchequer Bonds, Consols and Treasury Bills. In short, the times were against the launching of a new firm in a new industry.

While the war ended in 1902 there was no boom but in fact a mild depression until 1905, when the directors took heart and reorganised the company.

However the final comment should rest with the then Company Secretary of The Daimler Motor Company: 'If the directors of Lanchester had displayed a tenth of the abilities of F. W. they could have taken over Daimler.'

An Early Venture into
Self-Service

The Piggly Wiggly Stores
1919-1923

THIS IS the story of an early venture into American self-service grocery marketing, by Clarence Saunders, a plump, handsome man, and what can be perhaps justly described as the last of the Wall Street 'corners'.

The philosophy of the corner may be summed up in the old Wall Street jingle which goes, 'He who sells what isn't his'n must buy it back or go to prison.' The corner is a gamble, pure and simple, an aspect of the contest between bulls, who want the prices of stock to go up, and bears, who want it to go down. Legislation now makes the corner very difficult if not impossible to achieve but the bulls' basic method of operation was to buy stock, and the bears' to sell it. The average bear didn't own any of the stock issue in contest and so he resorted to the usual practice of 'selling short'. In other words the transaction is completed with stock that the seller has borrowed (at a suitable rate of interest) from a broker. Because brokers are only agents they in turn borrow the stock themselves from the pool which is in constant circulation among investment houses.

Put simply, the floating supply of stock consists of all that

in a particular company or corporation which is available
for trading and is not safely locked away somewhere. But
although the supply floats it is kept track of and the short
seller who may borrow a thousand shares from his broker
knows that he has incurred an immutable debt.

Of course, he hopes that the market price of the stock will
go down so that he can buy the shares he owes at a bargain
rate, pay off his debt and pocket the difference. His risk is
that the lender may demand that he delivers up his borrowed
shares at a time when the market price is high. To make
things even more hazardous in the days when corners were
posible on Wall Street the short seller had the additional strain
of dealing only with brokers. He was never told the identity
of the purchaser of his stock or the identity of the owner of
the stock he had borrowed.

Today, although condemned as being the tool of the
speculator, short selling is still sanctioned although in a severely
restricted form. In the 30s the US government outlawed any
short selling specifically intended to devitalise a stock. Other
rules in relation to manipulations virtually stopped the game
dead. Thus many financial experts say that Clarence Saunders
was the last intentional player of the game, the last of a long
and valiant line of American entrepreneurs.

Saunders was born in 1881 in Amherst County, Virginia,
and was employed by the local grocer as a lad. He soon went
on to a wholesale grocery company in Clarksville, Tennessee,
and then to one in Memphis.

While still in his 20s he organised a small retail food chain
called United Stores. He sold that after a few years, became
a wholesale grocer on his own and then, in 1919 began to
build a chain of retail self-service markets known as the Piggly
Wiggly Stores.

He soon became a well-known figure in Memphis and obtained slightly irrelevant fame for himself by embarking on
the building of the 'Pink Palace', an enormous house faced
with pink Georgia marble, in the grounds of which he planned
to have his own private golf course.

His stores flourished and by the autumn of 1922 there were over 1,200 of them. Of these rather more than half were owned outright by Piggly Wiggly Stores Inc, of which Saunders was the president and the rest were independently owned on a sort of franchise arrangement whereby the owners paid royalties to Piggly Wiggly for the right to adopt their patented method of operation and their name.

Saunders may have been the last man to have created a classic intentional corner in the US stock market; he was also one of the very first to introduce the self-service concept. Indeed it can be said that he invented the supermarket. In 1923 he even attracted the attention of the *New York Times*, in which their correspondent wrote:

'The customer in a Piggly Wiggly Store rambles down aisle after aisle, on both sides of which are shelves. The customer collects his purchases and pays as he goes out.'

In June 1922 the New York Stock Exchange began listing Piggly Wiggly and the stock soon achieved a reputation for being a solid if somewhat uninteresting investment.

However that situation did not last very long and in November 1922 several small companies that had been operating grocery stores in New York, New Jersey and Connecticut under the Piggly Wiggly name failed and went into liquidation. These companies were only franchisees of Saunders's company but their failures aroused the interest of a group of stock-market operators who immediately began a bear raid on the main company. They reasoned that if individual Piggly Wiggly stores were failing then the public could easily be led to believe that the parent firm was failing too. Without too much trouble stock could be bought cheap and then sold dear. So the operators began selling Piggly Wiggly short in order to force the price down. It yielded readily to their pressure and within a few weeks its price had dropped to below $40 a share instead of its summertime level of about $50.

Saunders was basically a company promoter, a knowledgeable and quite successful man in the grocery business. He was not in any sense a stock-manipulator or even an investor, except in his own company. But he was an energetic man and when he realised what was happening he announced to the press that he was going to 'beat the Wall Street professionals at their own game' with a buying campaign. He had every faith in Piggly Wiggly and he would back his faith with money. At the beginning of his campaign he certainly had no intention of trying for a corner—he was simply seeking to protect his own stock, his own investment and the investment of his shareholders.

Saunders was nothing if not a man of action and he supplemented his own funds with a loan of around 10 million dollars borrowed from a group of local bankers. The legend has followed him down the years—that he stuffed his $10 million-plus in notes of large denominations into a suitcase, boarded a train for New York and marched on Wall Street, ready to do battle for his company.

Whether this story is true or not (Saunders afterwards denied it) he did speedily get some 20 brokers onto his side.

On the first day of his war against the stock market operators Saunders, operating through his brokers, bought 33,000 shares of Piggly Wiggly, mostly from the short sellers. Within a week he had upped this to 105,000 or more than half of the 200,000 shares floating on the market. At the same time he started a series of advertisements attacking Wall Street speculators. His language was heated and flamboyant. His copy went something like this:

'Shall the gambler rule? On a white horse he rides. Bluff is his coat of mail and thus shielded is a yellow heart. His helmet is deceit, his spurs clink with treachery, and the hoof-beats of his horse thunder destruction. Shall good business flee? Shall it tremble with fear? Shall it be the loot of the speculator?'

Saunders's buying campaign was successful. By late January 1923 he had driven the price of the stock up to over $60, higher than ever before. No doubt the stock-market operators who had started it all were wishing they had never touched Piggly Wiggly or this energetic country boy. To intensify their alarm reports now came from the Chicago Stock Exchange that Piggly Wiggly was cornered—short sellers could not replace the stock they had borrowed without coming to Saunders for supplies. These reports were promptly denied by the New York Stock Exchange which put out an announcement that the floating supply of Piggly Wiggly was ample but the rumour that a corner did exist—prematurely—may well have put the germ of an idea into Saunders's head.

In February 1923 he made an odd move: his regular newspaper advertisements were changed and he offered to *sell* 50,000 shares of Piggly Wiggly stock to the public at $55 a share. The advertisement pointed out that the return was more than 7% per annum. Unfettered by any later·restrictions on investment advertising Saunders was able to end his copy:

'To get in on the ground floor of any big proposition is the opportunity that comes to few, and then only once in a lifetime.' But this was only a pale shadow of what was to follow. How, the next advertisements were to ask, can Clarence Saunders be so generous to the public and in a remarkable effusion he likened himself to Daniel, uneaten by the lions, Joseph answering the riddles, and Moses born to a new promised land.

Why indeed was Saunders being so generous? Many thought he was exceedingly foolish because when he was busily offering shares at $55 the price on the New York Stock Exchange was rising swiftly to very nearly $70.

There was in fact a catch. Saunders was not simply making a costly and unbusinesslike offer but, a rank novice at the stock exchange game, he had in fact devised a very crafty dodge. One of the great hazards in a corner is that the winner might in fact have no victory at all. It was a question of knowing when to stop. Once the short sellers had been squeezed dry the cornerer might find that he had acquired stacks of stock which were a millstone around his neck. Then he was in a dilemma because if he pushed it back into the market quickly the price would go down even more speedily. If, like Saunders, he had borrowed heavily to bid for the corner at all he was at very great risk. Settlement day would come; his creditors would demand their just dues and not only strip him of his gains but drive him into bankruptcy.

Saunders with the cunning of the untutored was shrewd enough to anticipate this hazard just as soon as he realised he was beginning to create a corner and very cleverly he made plans to unload some of his stock *before* winning, instead of afterwards. But he had to prevent the stock he was selling going back into the floating supply because if he allowed this his corner would be promptly broken. So his advertisements offered to sell his $55 shares on a deposit and instalment system. Prospective buyers *had* to pay in instalments, even if they were eager and able to put cash down.

Saunders stipulated that the only way the public could buy the shares was to pay $25 down and the balance in three $10 instalments due on 1 June, 1 September and 1 December 1923 and, quite properly, he refused to turn over the stock certificates to the buyers until the final payment had been made. As the buyers couldn't sell the certificates until they had them no stock could be used to replenish the floating supply until early in December, which gave him plenty of time to squeeze the short sellers dry.

Put like this it is easy to appreciate Saunders's plan but it was so unorthodox that the governors of the New York Stock Exchange could not fathom out what was happening and they ordered an inquiry. Meanwhile the brokers went on buying on Saunders's account and succeeded in pushing Piggly Wiggly up well above $70. And he went on offering the stock at $55.

While the New York Stock Exchange governors could not quite make out all the implications of all that Saunders was doing it was pretty obvious he was trying for a corner. Having 20 brokers working on his behalf Saunders had appointed one of them overall manager. He was Jessel Livermore who was one of the celebrated American speculators of this century. In 1908, when he was only 20, he had lost almost a million dollars trying to get a corner in cotton and had earned himself the title of 'Boy Plunger'. With such unhappy memories Livermore was now, understandably, losing his nerve and he called Saunders to a conference in March 1923. After lengthy discussions Livermore bowed out of the operation and Saunders, nothing daunted, decided to run it for himself.

A week later, in the middle of March, Saunders had his corner. He claimed he had acquired all but 1,128 of Piggly Wiggly's 200,000 outstanding shares, some of which he owned and the rest of which he 'controlled', the latter being the instalment-plan shares, the certificates for which he still held. In spite of his break with Livermore, Saunders now thought it time to act and asked the broker if he would like to call, on his behalf, for all the shares that were owed to him. Livermore turned this suggestion down so on Tuesday 20 March Saunders sprang the trap himself.

On that historic day Piggly Wiggly opened at $75\frac{1}{2}$, up $5\frac{1}{2}$ from the previous day's closing price, speedily ran to 124 but fell to 82 by the time the Exchange's closing bell ended what must have been a chaotic session.

It was a crowded day, too. An hour after the opening it was announced that Saunders had called for delivery of all his stock. According to the Exchange rules stock called for under such circumstances had to be produced by 2.15 the following afternoon but, of course, as Saunders well knew there wasn't much stock to be had. Frantic short sellers fastened on the very few shares still held by private investors and one lucky man who had bought 1,100 shares at 39 in the previous autumn unloaded at 105 and collected for himself a profit of over $70,000.

As the day wore on desperate short sellers bought up what Piggly Wiggly they could lay their hands on at 90, then at 100, then at 110. By after lunch the stock had risen to 124 and brokers were predicting it would reach a dizzy 200 before the end of the day. This was not to be, however, because the news came through that the governors of the Exchange were meeting to consider the suspension of further trading in the stock and the postponement of the short sellers' deadline for delivery. If this happened and the bears were given time Saunders's corner would be weakened if not broken. So it was that on the basis of this rumour Piggly Wiggly fell to 82 by the end of the session.

The rumour was in fact correct. Following the close of business the Governing Committee of the Exchange suspended trading and extended the short sellers' deadline for an unspecified time.

Until this event Saunders had been extremely lucky and very, very shrewd considering he knew so little about stock exchange procedure. But now he did not realise the extent to which his position had been undermined and that while he was on paper a dollar millionaire several times over, it was only on paper. On Wednesday he gave a series of boastful interviews to the press declaring how the 'boob from Tennessee' had licked 'the boastful and supposedly invulnerable Wall Street powers'. And he wound up his interview with an astonishing demand : notwithstanding the Stock Exchange's deadline he expected settlement in full on all short stock by 3 pm on Thursday at $150 a share. Thereafter his price would be $250.

Few came forward on the Thursday and on the same day the Stock Exchange announced that the stock of Piggly Wiggly was permanently removed from its trading list and that the short sellers would be given until 2.15 the following Monday to meet their obligations. The horrible implications of this delay were probably not entirely apparent to Saunders, but he saw, quite clearly, that things were moving against him. Resorting to the press again he found it 'unbelieveable' that the 'august and all-powerful New York Stock Exchange is a welcher'. The Memphis local press backed him up, crying treachery by the city slickers. And on the same day, purely by coincidence, the annual balance sheet of Piggly Wiggly Stores

G

Inc was made public. It recorded a very good year: sales, profits, current assets, all were up. But, sadly, nobody took any notice. The real worth of the company had long been forgotten in the welter of share dealings.

On Friday morning Saunders lost his nerve and said that he would settle up for $100 per share. He had little alternative. The postponement granted by the Stock Exchange would give the short sellers and their brokers a chance to go right through the lists of Piggly Wiggly stockholders with a toothcomb. There they found small blocks of shares that Saunders had not cornered and most of the small investors who held them were only too happy to sell, especially as they could no longer be traded on the Exchange. Most of them got about twice the price they had paid, which at any rate is pleasant to record. So instead of having to buy stock from Saunders at his previous price of $250 and then hand it back to him in settlement of loans a large percentage of the short sellers were able to buy it in over the counter and pay off Saunders not in cash but in shares of Piggly Wiggly—the very last thing he wanted just then, being almost literally up to his neck in the stores' stock. By the evening of Friday nearly all the short sellers were in the clear, having purchased, or reluctantly paid Saunders cash at $100 a share.

Saunders sought out the press again, and announced 'Of all the institutions in America, the New York Stock Exchange is the worst menace of all in its power to ruin all who dare to oppose it. A law unto itself . . . an association of men who claim the right that no king or autocrat ever dare to take: to make a rule that applies one day on contracts and abrogate it the next day to let out a bunch of welchers.'

The Exchange was sufficiently moved by this and other of Saunders's accusations to publish a lengthy review on the crisis from the beginning to the end. The Exchange stressed the public harm that might have been done if the corner had gone unbroken.

But all this was beside the point to Saunders. He was in a desperate financial situation. Admittedly a wave of public sympathy ran through the country and even the *New York Times* made public the widespread belief that Saunders was St George and the Stock Exchange the dragon.

Saunders went busily to work on this sympathy. He certainly needed to do something. When he had paid his bankers the money he had received from the short sellers and from his public stock sale he still owed about $5 million, half of it due on 1 September 1923 and the balance on 1 January 1924. He had, of course, a huge bundle of Piggly Wiggly shares in his possession but he could no longer sell them on the Exchange. So he began his advertising campaign again supplemented with direct mail and once again he made his offer at $55 per share. But sympathy was one thing and cash another. The papers had screamed about Piggly Wiggly for several weeks and very few people were prepared to take the risk and put their money down.

Not entirely dismayed Saunders next appealed to Tennessee. He sought to convince Memphis and the cities around that his financial dilemma was a civic issue. If he went into bankruptcy, he argued, it would besmirch Southern honour. As he said, 'For Piggly Wiggly to be ruined would shame the whole South.'

Saunders was nothing if not a large spender on advertising and soon the *Memphis Commercial Appeal*, the local newspaper, was vigorously urging the town to back up their local boy. Suddenly the business leaders planned a three-day campaign with the object of selling 50,000 shares of his stock to the citizens of Memphis at $55 a share. But so that nobody should feel that they were buying unsupported stock it was made a condition that unless the whole block was sold within three days all sales would be null and void. At this point Saunders must have warmed to Memphis. The Chamber of Commerce, the American Legion, the Civatan Club and the Exchange Club all sponsored the drive and, even more heartening, competitive grocers in Memphis gave their backing. Hundreds of volunteers agreed to ring door bells and to sell the shares.

As a prelude to the campaign 250 Memphis businessmen assembled in the local hotel for a send-off dinner. When Saunders entered the room, accompanied by his wife, he got a standing ovation. The after-dinner speakers were long and fulsome. One described him as 'The man who has done more· for Memphis than any in the last thousand years.' Supporting the event the *Commercial Appeal* wrote poetically, 'Business rivalries and personal differences were swept away like mists before the sun.'

On the opening day, 8 May 1923, hundreds of people paraded the streets of Memphis wearing badges 'We're One Hundred Per Cent for Clarence Saunders and Piggly Wiggly'. Windows showed compelling slogans, 'A Share of Piggly Wiggly Stock in Every Home.'

Before the end of the first day nearly half of the 50,000 shares had been subscribed. And then something odd happened. Rumours started and a request came that Saunders consent to an immediate spot audit of his company's books. Saunders—and it is difficult to see the reason—refused, but offered to step down as president of Piggly Wiggly if it would help the campaign. He was not asked to do this but on the second day a committee of four—three bankers and a business-man—were appointed by Saunders' co-directors to help him run the company for an interim period while passions cooled. Then some more doubts arose. Somebody pointed out that building work was continuing on Saunders's million-dollar Pink Palace just at the time everybody was working for him for nothing. In all probability Saunders had been so busy that he had not had any time to issue instructions and the builders had gone on working automatically to their original brief but Saunders replied hastily that he would have them called off the very next day and there would be no further construction work.

However the damage was done and the drive slowly ground to a halt. On the second and third day hardly any shares were sold at all and the sales that had been made were cancelled.

Unable to sell Piggly Wiggly stock Saunders turned his

attention to the stores and started selling them off piecemeal, partly liquidating the company. The Chicago stores went first and then those in Denver and Kansas City followed. By June he believed that he had got Wall Street 'licked' but in mid-August, now very close to the 1 September deadline, he resigned as President and turned over his assets—his stock in the company, his Pink Palace, and all the rest of his assets, to his creditors.

Shares were going now at a dollar each and early in 1924 Saunders was forced into formal bankruptcy proceedings. So ended Piggly Wiggly.

But not Saunders. He no longer owned the Pink Palace— it eventually came into the hands of Memphis who turned it into a museum of natural history and industrial arts—but in 1928 he started a new grocery chain, the full title of which was the Clarence Saunders, Sole Owners of My Name Stores Inc, but which soon became known as Sole Owner Stores. Saunders may have not been clever enough for the New York financiers but he was an experienced grocer and he rose again, very rapidly, and was soon able to buy a million-dollar estate just outside Memphis. At the same time, after almost complete eclipse, the Piggly Wiggly Stores under new management was also struggling upwards again. Indeed with a completely changed corporate structure it flourishes to this day and there are hundreds of Piggly Wiggly stores throughout the States, now operated under a franchise agreement with the Piggly Wiggly Corporation of Jacksonville, Florida.

Unfortunately Saunders's second essay into glory was more fleeting. The depression hit Sole Owner Stores heavily and in 1930 he went bankrupt for the second time. But Saunders had guts and an inventive mind. His original venture into self-service was far before its time. Now, after his last bankruptcy, he planned a new chain of grocery stores—the Keedoozle.

This was an electrically operated grocery store. Merchandise was displayed behind glass panels, each with a slot beside it, rather like the American Automat. But instead of inserting coins in the slot to open a panel and lift out a purchase customers inserted a key that they were given on entering the store. Each time the key was inserted in the slot the identity of the item selected was inscribed in code on a segment of recording tape embedded in the key itself and the item was automatically transferred to a conveyor belt which carried it to an exit gate at the front of the store. When a customer had finished her shopping she presented her key to a cashier at the exit, who deciphered the tape and added up the bill. When this was paid the purchases, bagged and wrapped, were waiting for the customer at the end of the conveyor belt.

Who knows, such an idea may become practical in the future. Clarence Saunders was always quite a few years ahead of his times, although two pilot stores, one in Memphis and the other in Chicago never worked very well. Nothing daunted, he turned his inventive mind to the Foodelectric which did everything the Keedoozle could do but added up the bill as well, thus dispensing with the cashiers. This latest brainchild was still unfinished when Saunders died in October 1953.

The Fall of the 'Karpet King of Europe'

The House of Lord
1945-1969

ALMOST single-handed Cyril Lord changed the entire character of the British carpet industry, transforming it from a cottage operation to a successful mass market venture. He built Europe's largest and best equipped tufted carpet factory and sold more than any other manufacturer. In August 1966, only 18 months after Lord had gone public, he turned in record profits for the second year running.

Then, in November 1969, the company collapsed, owing some £5 million. His executives, salesmen, agents, secretaries, typists—all lost their jobs. One hire purchase company which had backed him heavily was forced to close down and a number of advertising agencies and other suppliers were more than a little upset.

Before Lord ever went into carpets he had made a name and fortune for himself in textiles. Born in 1911 in a Lancashire cotton mill village, the son of a Co-operative Movement employee who retired as a coal manager, he was fascinated by textiles from an early age and took up an apprenticeship in a local textile company.

Quite soon afterwards he was involved in the design and

manufacture of 'artificial silk'—rayon in continuous filament form—and he constructed cloths which were in his own phrase 'definitely different' and which caught the public eye.

After graduating from the Manchester College of Technology he joined a London company in 1931. Lord's objective now was to put his name over to women buying materials by the yard and in this he was extremely successful, in spite of all the problems which the textile industry suffered between the wars and in particular the competition from Japan.

Lord had one difference from the average entrepreneur whose activities have entertained us since the end of the war : he was not only a very successful and spectacular salesman but he was also a master of the technical mysteries of his industry. From his early days as a laboratory assistant in Manchester Lord mastered the complexities of the very sophisticated machines which had been introduced between the wars. In 1952 his growing reputation was recognised by Burlington Industries, the largest textile group in the world, who summoned him to the States to help them sort out a problem they were having in producing new fashion fabrics from artificial fibres. Lord succeeded. He was also awarded an Honorary Doctorate by the University of California's Advanced College of Textile Technology and later made Chancellor of Florida Southern College for his work 'in the sphere of international textiles'.

By 1953 the Lancashire textile business, with all its complications and complexities, had made Lord a millionaire since he had begun to work for himself less than 10 years earlier. Then, in the spring of 1954, he started to seriously consider carpets. And it was about that time that Stanley Shorrock, the Managing Director of a small Blackburn-based company called British Tufting Machinery received a call from Lord's Production Director, a young Lancashire textile engineer, Ian Brackall.

For Shorrock this was a potentially important meeting because since 1952 he had been trying to persuade the carpet and textile companies to buy an entirely new type of machinery which he had modified from an American design. This was the 'tufting machine' expected to radically change and cheapen the carpet-making process. Instead of weaving the pile into the backing by conventional methods the new machines did not really weave at all. On each was mounted a bar carrying hundreds of needles which thrust individual strands of yarn into a backing material and cut off the strand at the same time. To prevent the yarn tufts falling out again a second backing was stuck to the first with glue or latex. The principle had already been used in the manufacture of candlewick bedspreads in the States but until an inventor in Chattanooga, Tennessee designed the tufting machine nobody had thought of making carpets by this method.

Lord had heard about the Chattanooga machine, quickly saw its possibilities, and flew to the States. However, he was not alone in his perception. John Crossley, Carpet Manufacturing, Brintons and Templetons also saw the possibilities and banded together to form Kosset, a company which was to exploit the potential of tufted carpets. Lancaster Carpet was also showing an interest and when Lord chose British Tufting's machine in preference to the Chattanooga machine several small companies had already bought before him.

But Lord was thinking bigger than all of them put together and he realised all the potentials. Not only could a tufted carpet be made in about a twentieth of the time it took to make a Wilton or an Axminster, but it could also be done with unskilled labour. The price of a tufted carpet was further reduced because it was made from synthetic fibre; in fact it had to be because the machines demanded very even strands of yarn which only the synthetics could provide.

Early would-be manufacturers came to grief because uncrimped rayon was found to be quite unsuitable for carpet manufacture and it was not until the arrival of nylon and crimped rayon that the market became really practical.

At the time of the Lord collapse Shorrocks revealed to Stephen Aris and Brian Moynihan of the *Sunday Times* just

how big Lord was thinking in this new venture. Brackall, his
Production Director, 'asked me to draw up plans for a tufted
plant with a capacity of 100,000 sq yds a week. He wanted to
know how big a factory should be, what type of machinery
should be used and exactly where it should be positioned. I
was given just 40 minutes to do the job. I've never worked so
fast : 40 minutes later I gave him a piece of paper sketching
out what later became the Donaghadee factory.'

A week later Shorrock and Brackall flew to Northern
Ireland where they inspected what was to be the largest
tufted carpet factory in the world—the site at that time was
typically wet Irish fields given over to grazing.

With typical Lord hustle the huge factory was completed by
the end of 1956 and Lord Brookebrough, the then Prime
Minister of Northern Ireland, laid the foundation stone. The
next year the first carpet rolled off the line and in Stephen
Aris's and Brian Moynihan's words, 'the second and most
dramatic phase of Lord's career began.' Needless to say Lord's
plans had been received with great enthusiasm by the Government of Northern Ireland; bedevilled then as now with un-
employment they were glad to make him a 21-year loan of
£2,790,000.

This was not Lord's first introduction to the textile workers
of Northern Ireland and from previous experience he admired
them greatly for their hardworking qualities.

Following his experience at the London firm of Scott and
Son, which was both textile wholesales and merchant converters, he had started his own converting firm on a shoestring
in August 1939. Despite the war following almost immediately
it was enough of a success for him to sell it the following year
and he then joined the Cotton Board as an adviser. The
Board's task was to organise and administer the Government's
utility scheme and to ration the small supplies of yarn available to the manufacturers as fairly as possible. Quite soon after
Lord joined the Board he was sent by Sir Thomas Barlow,
who was then its chairman, to Northern Ireland.

Here the industry was in a serious condition. The weaving

and spinning of flax was one of Northern Ireland's basic industries but both mills and converters were having great difficulty in keeping going because of the shortage of raw materials. The Cotton Board devised the idea of teaching the flax men to weave synthetics because flax was in such short supply. The flax weavers had never handled artificial fibres before and they found it very difficult to adapt to the new conditions and techniques of handling the long-fibre viscose yarns demanded by the utility specification.

Lord spent four years in Northern Ireland teaching them and co-ordinating their production. At the end of this period his reputation as a technical man had been made, he had made valuable contacts with the raw material suppliers and, perhaps most important of all, they provided him with a source of capital for post-war development. The Bank of Ireland was particularly impressed with the way in which Lord had set the Northern Irish weavers on their feet and promised him help if he decided to open up in Lancashire when the war ended. This connection also smoothed the way for the new venture, the carpet factory at Donaghadee.

Following the end of the war Lord with William McMillan (a Belfast solicitor) started to buy their way into Lancashire with the help of the Bank of Ireland, one of whose directors, the late Lord Glenavy, came on to Lord's Board. At any other time this might have been difficult because of the closely-knit family traditions of the Lancashire textile industry but, heavily bruised by the war, there were a number of mill-owning families anxious to sell.

In February 1949 Lord became a mill-owner for the first time and bought a small private company with two weaving mills at Chorley. It was called Brindles and it cost him £120,000. A few months later he bought another mill at Leyland and only two years afterwards Lord and McMillan entered the big time stakes by buying three spinning mills, two at Lily Mill and one at Devon Mill for £1,195,000.

These were profitable investments and between 1945 when Lord returned to the textile trade as a merchant converter and

1954 when he went public the pre-tax profits rose from £381 to £517,000. His shares were put on the market by the Ocean Trust and, such was the confidence of the public in Lord, that they were 12 times oversubscribed.

By then Lord was contemplating his carpet project but it was not announced to the public invited to subscribe for the shares. Undoubtedly he sought diversification because at that time Lancashire was going through one of its periodically bad periods, faced with the competition of Japanese and Indian cotton. The year was in fact one of the worst in its history and while 90% of the industry's looms were busily at work in January of that year by December only 60% were operative. Energetic Lord was vociferous in lobbying the government of the day for 100% protection for the cotton industry and over the next few years his hefty broadsides against the government, and most particularly the Board of Trade, got him almost as much publicity as his new ventures.

Lord might be a very competent technical man; he was also an expert publicist and got up to all sorts of tricks to put over the cause of the Lancashire mill-owners. For example, he took a half page advertisement in the *Financial Times* 'To state the case for Lancashire'; he passed himself off as a journalist and heckled a junior Board of Trade Minister at a press conference; he sent cotton spindles to all Members of Parliament, peers and industrialists and followed this up with wallets full of Japanese money, gramophone records and pieces of cloth bearing pictures of grinning Japanese. Nevertheless Lord failed in his objective, although it is possible that his activities did something to speed the Cotton Industry Act 1959, which enabled the industry to re-equip on a massive scale.

However, in spite of Lord's brilliant publicity, mills closed down steadily all over Lancashire and as he himself became more and more involved in carpets his own mills closed, too. By 1965 when his group went fully public weaving had almost been eliminated and the spinning was concentrated at Manchester and Rochdale. There were still five companies in the textile business but not all of them were operating and they were all losing money—as compared with profits of around £500,000 ten years earlier.

But although Lord was becoming more and more involved in carpets (he lost £17,000 in the first two years but made a profit of £273,000 in the third) he could not bring himself to abandon textiles altogether and in 1962 he announced his decision to move the bulk of his textile business, equipment and employees, to South Africa. He projected a £750,000 poplin factory in a Bantu area just outside East London. Apart from the senior management and 400 skilled workers, who were to be flown out from England, his work force was to be wholly black and the start in production was projected for late in 1963.

Following the signature of the agreement with the South African Development Corporation the entire contents of Devon Mill and Kew Mill was dismantled and shipped. Closely following the machinery came the employees who arrived in June 1963 on board the 'Cyril Lord Special', three Boeing 707s which had been chartered for the occasion.

But Lord had failed to do his homework (a failing which led eventually to his complete downfall). The East London factory had been going for only a few months when it became obvious to the Directors of Cyril Lord (SA) Pty Ltd that their South African advisers had grossly over-estimated the demand for poplin. The company had been advised that there was a market for 30 million square yards whereas the true figure was nearer 16 million square yards. Furthermore, the South African poplin importers, well warned of Lord's arrival by his usual dramatic publicity methods, had stockpiled heavily—so heavily that 18 months after Cyril Lord (SA) began production the importers still had a year's excess stock of imported poplin.

Even worse, Lord had started up some vigorous local competition. Five other South African manufacturers were busily manufacturing poplin. By 1964 South Africa must have stockpiled enough poplin to keep the world going for the best part of a year.

In 1965 the factory was forced to stop all spinning and weaving of unfinished 'grey' poplin and parts of the combing plant were completely shut down. Production was switched to calico and linens.

Barely 18 months after the opening of the factory the South Africans stepped in, taking over the management and injecting more cash. It was not until December of 1968 that the first profit was recorded but Lord, who originally had a 50% stake had by then reduced his holding to 8%.

At the time this fiasco led to considerable City comment and some criticism of Lord and his co-directors. It was also a pointer to the weakness of the Lord empire which many believe eventually brought about its downfall. Lord, with his usual ebullient enthusiasm had taken the word of the South Africans for the size of the market and for its profitability. But surely any businessman going into such a large venture should have done his own market research? A very small sum expended in this direction would have quickly revealed the true state of the market. Lord had successfully weathered many crises in the textile industry; by the 60s he was perhaps a shade over-confident, too ready to back his own judgment regardless of facts presented to him by his colleagues and too insensitive to the market as a whole. Several of these misjudgments and the whole of the Lord empire was in deep trouble. Lord, bustling and enormously energetic, charged everything with the same sense of urgency but sometimes a little quiet thought and research might have been more productive.

Stephen Aris and Brian Moynihan have told two stories about the Donaghadee factory which, true or not, perfectly illustrate Lord's character.

The first is about the time when Donaghadee was being built. One Sunday evening in the summer of 1955 the Heysham-Belfast Ferry was steaming across the Irish Sea on its normal run when a speedboat came into view, travelling fast. As it came closer the passengers could see a bald, tubby man at the wheel and on the bow, in large blue and white letters, was the name *Sea Lord*. (Lord had a passion for powerful speedboats and had got through about six, all of them with the same name, by the time the House of Lord had fallen.) As the distance between the ferry and *Sea Lord* closed the little man picked up a megaphone and shouted 'I'm Cyril Lord, where the hell are my girders?'

This particular story is apocryphal; Lord has denied it and nobody else can recall the incident. Yet it is very true of the man.

The other story concerns the time when the company went public and the senior partner from Warburgs, the merchant bankers, arrived in Donaghadee to discuss the operation—which in the end this bank did not handle. The partner did not arrive until around midnight and no doubt was looking forward only to a good night's sleep before he started work in the morning. But Lord was too impatient for that and the unfortunate banker was taken straight from the plane for an immediate tour of the factory.

Nevertheless, in spite of the South African episode Lord's carpet enterprises were enormously successful. His techniques were not unlike those adopted by Bloom of Rolls Razor discussed elsewhere in this book. Like Bloom, Lord by-passed the wholesaler, spent lavishly on advertising and vigorously followed up a coupon response to these advertisements. He also spent a small fortune on television and his progress is reflected by the company's advertising budget. In 1958, a year after he had gone into carpets seriously he spent just under £50,000; in 1966 when his fortunes and reputation were at their height he was spending only a little below £800,000. Courtaulds and British Enkalon, who supplied the bulk of Lord's fibre, were co-operating in this exercise but nevertheless his budget was still four times as much as that of his nearest competitor, Kosset.

It was in 1967 that he was officially crowned 'Karpet King of Europe' by none other than Batman. At that time British youngsters were being entertained in the afternoons with the series 'Ice Spy', an American production featuring Batman and his boy assistant, Robin. One afternoon these two intrepid

characters were climbing a skyscraper in pursuit of the Awful
Mister Freeze. As Batman and Robin approached the top a
window opened and a head appeared—the head of none other
than Cyril Lord.

'Who's that?' Robin asked.

'Why,' Batman replied, 'don't you know, that's the Karpet
King of Europe?'

And, as Robin so rightly replied, 'Holy Matman.'

It was a title that he had really earned: his energetic promotion of tufted carpets had changed the floors of Europe;
masses of people who even in the relative affluence of the
sixties were linoleum orientated had succumbed to Lord car-
peting. For the first time since the war working-class newly-
weds could contemplate the ultimate luxury, the fitted carpet,
without unduly straining their budget.

In August 1966 with record profits under his belt Lord
could say to his shareholders: 'In the long term I feel confident that with the increasing acceptance of tufted carpets we
must go from strength to strength. In the short term, barring
the incidence of a deep depression in the economy and further
government interference with home consumption demand, the
same remarks apply.'

And in the short term Lord's confidence seemed to be entirely justified. A month after his speech to the shareholders
sales were $12\frac{1}{2}\%$ up on the corresponding period of the previous year and the company had a 30% share of the market.

South Africa had been an annoying but not fatal mistake;
unfortunately others were to follow. In 1963, indeed, he had
also made a comparatively minor error of judgment. In that
year he went to Russia on a goodwill mission led by Lord
Thomson and was greatly impressed by a machine which the
Russians had developed for making artificial astrakhan. Lord
returned complete with astrakhan hat and immediately sent
Ian Brackall, the Production Director, over to Moscow to
examine the machine in detail. Brackall reported that from
the production and engineering point of view the machine
was perfectly satisfactory and the company bought two for

£36,000 (partly subsidised by the Northern Ireland Government) and installed them at Donaghadee.

But it was some time before his London Harley Street sales office and headquarters (housed where Florence Nightingale had once lived) even got to know about the new machines and when they did their information was somewhat fragmentary. As in South Africa there was no proper market research and no one knew the market for imitation astrakhan and the Persian Lamb that the machines had been bought to manufacture. As a consequence when the firm crashed the output of astrakhan and Persian Lamb was precisely nil. Here, in spite of his flare for publicity, Lord showed himself overwhelmingly production rather than marketing orientated. It is probably not unfair to say that he was so taken by the excellence of the machines that he forgot entirely that the product must be sold.

Much more disastrous to the company was the vinyl flooring venture, an attempt by Lord to diversify and break into a completely new area of the flooring market. His decision to do this is extremely difficult to understand because it did not need even elementary market research for him to be aware that in the mid-sixties over-capacity in this area was rife, there was price cutting on every side, many failures, and for those who survived uneconomically low profits. There was also the fact that Marley Tile had most of the market that was worth having.

In spite of this Lord wasted no time in ordering the largest vinyl machine in Britain, which was capable of producing the flooring in 12 ft widths. This went into Donaghadee and Lord announced 'The biggest floor show on earth'.

But if he had failed to research sufficiently the state of the market it was also necessary to undertake technical research before the machine could go into production. What was the thin vinyl to be backed with? Traditionally asbestos was the material but the Lord vinyl machine was so wide that no asbestos manufacturer could help him. Other alternatives discussed were jute, paper and polypropylene, but these were either unacceptable to the trade or technically indefensible. In

H

the event Lord's vinyl flooring never went on the market and an enormous sum was lost on machinery and development.

Afterwards Marley confessed that they had never been seriously worried, believing that Lord had been misled by delusions of grandeur. Marley's Frederick Hardy, quoted by Stephen Aris and Brian Moynihan said, 'The trade wouldn't touch the 12 ft stuff. The buyer can't put it in the boot of his car and drive off with it. We started with 4 ft strips with cars very much in mind. There is now an excellent demand for 6 ft widths but how many English bathrooms and kitchens will take 12 ft? This isn't the States.'

Other errors of judgment, insufficient research, too much enthusiasm for the grand gesture, revealed themselves after the collapse. For example, in the new seven-storey office block at Rathgael, which was built just before the debacle, there was a highly sophisticated computer-controlled storage system which cost around £100,000. Norwegian made, it was one of the most expensive and elaborate systems then available but what Lord and his executives apparently failed to understand was that, impressive though it might be, it was ineffective as a device for handling carpets. In theory a roll of carpet was selected by the computer from the store, moved to the cutting tables, chopped to size and then, apparently, left where it fell because there was no system of putting the roll back into the store. Thus after all the automation the rolls had to be man-handled.

Production extravagances of this sort, the vinyl and the astrakhan projects were not in themselves disastrous but they certainly did not help the overall prosperity of the company. Then a third, famous and very serious mistake occurred.

On one of his trips to America Lord had visited the famous Astrodome, 'the largest covered area in the world', and found in the Texans kindred spirits who, like Lord, loved to do things on a big scale. Lord was fascinated by the 'grass' of the baseball pitch which was in fact a genuine, 100%, carpet, woven and coloured in such a way that it looked exactly like grass.

Brackall was immediately despatched to investigate and discussions with Monsanto followed. Lord adapted machinery in a considerable development programme and ordered new synthetic materials. He decided to call his new baby 'Cyrilawn'. Predictably the publicity was enormous and, by the spring of 1967, it appeared that the technical problems had been overcome. Already there had been a check because the Astrodome turf was woven while, of course, Cyrilawn had to be tufted but now Lord declared that the launch could take place.

The launching party at the London Hilton was lavish by any standards and cost the company some £6,000. The entire ballroom was converted into a miniature Wimbledon and more than 400 guests were invited to watch Hardie Amies, Barbara Kelly, the Marquess of Dufferin and Ava and Reginald Maudling playing tennis on an immaculate stretch of Cyrilawn. This was a brilliant public relations exercise and was a huge success.

But again something seemed to be going wrong with the company's judgment. It is one of the most obvious precepts of public relations that you don't create a demand for something which doesn't exist and in fact, in spite of the elaborate publicity which appeared in the press the next day, and the many serious enquiries which resulted, there was indeed no product. Incredible but true. It seems as if Lord's executives could not keep up with his boundless energy and the rapidity with which he fired off ideas. Yet dynamic, bustling little Lord was popular with his colleagues and employees; he was in no sense a despot although his judgment was never challenged. Perhaps the Lord image of infallibility overcame all his executives' critical faculties.

In the event, perhaps the delay in production was just as well because as the months went by the technicians at Donaghadee noticed that Cyrilawn was changing colour. Gradually the grass green began to fade and odd patches of blue appeared, apparently caused by a chemical instability in the special dye that had been used. Faced with this problem the research department showed a curious ineptitude and did not seem to be able to grasp that the changes considerably reduced the commercial attractions of their product. Stephen Aris and Brian Moynihan report that to one salesman who wrote to complain they replied : 'Don't worry. In course of time the green will disappear and the entire carpet will turn blue.

The change of colour was not all that went wrong with Cyrilawn. It also seemed to gather a curious, repellent slime. In the course of the promotion the company had presented Queen's Club, ranking second only to Wimbledon in prestige, with the tennis court covering that had been used at the Hilton. Because the slime developed the embarrassed secretary offered later to give it back to Lord but the company refused. By that time they had 100,000 sq yds of their own lying unsold.

Apart from errors of judgment in production techniques, which would have sapped the resources of the company but which would not have been known to a wide public, South Africa, the astrakhan venture, vinyl and now Cyrilawn had all done their bit to damage the credibility of the Lord empire. Cyrilawn in particular set people talking. But worse was to follow.

In the spring of 1967, only six months after the firm had reported record profits, the broking firm of Sir R. W. Carden & Macnicoll called on the company. This broking firm had been one of the first to back Lord's entry into the carpet market and had persuaded some of their best and largest clients, including two pension fund managers, to invest. Thus it was the brokers' duty to keep the company under close and continuous scrutiny. In particular they wanted to know why the latest profit forecast had been revised downwards by £200,000 in October 1966, just two months after the record figures had been issued. Originally the enquiry had been directed to Northern Ireland but the management there, led by Ian Brackall had explained that they were unable to help because production was their concern. Thus the brokers went to Cyril Lord and William McMillan, who had now been associated with Lord for over 20 years.

The brokers also wanted to know why Lord was opening so many retail shops, why so much was being spent on advertising and what steps was he taking to meet increasing competition. All these enquiries were started by the issuing of a new £1¼ million debenture, which seemed curious to the brokers when the balance sheet indicated that there was sufficient money inside the company for its needs.

Lord and McMillan did their best to reassure the brokers but they went away not entirely happy. In their comments afterwards they put their finger on a weakness which is the main reason for some of the disastrous judgments already noted. They said: 'We were always a little nervous of this company. It was such a complete one-man band.'

When the results for the half year came in at the end of August 1967 everyone connected with the company were in for a great shock. The pre-tax profits for the second half of the financial year from December 1966 to May 1967 were not £636,000 as had been forecast originally; they were not even the guaranteed minimum level of £412,000, about which Lord and McMillan had talked so reassuringly. In fact profits had taken a tremendous dive to a mere £46,000.

Inevitably the results produced a tremendous reaction and brokers interested in the company wanted explanations from Lord and McMillan. But they were both on holiday: Lord in the West Indies and McMillan in Majorca. The brokers, like the shareholders, had to wait for Lord's return and the annual general meeting for an explanation. There Lord said: 'Carpet sales increases in January and February gave cause for optimism but they were not maintained in the usually heavy sales months of March, April and May and they finished the year with a reduction of 6%.' But this was hardly an explanation. If sales had dropped by 6% how did profits fall by 93% on the forecast?

We have already mentioned the apparent complacency of Lord's executives when faced with an increasingly unsatisfactory situation. How much they raised objections it is almost impossible to say because the brokers previously quoted had put their finger on the shortcoming: the Lord empire was a one-man band.

Expenditure was also racing ahead wildly, it seemed. Apart from all the mistakes, apart from the abortive computer set-up already mentioned, a 250,000 sq ft production area had been added to Donaghadee at a cost of £250,000; a new and luxurious office block had just been completed at Rathgael and a new and expensive spinning and printing unit had been set up—apparently without any reference to the production executives at Donaghadee, because it simply arrived one morning out of the blue. The comments, if any, of Lord's executives from the beginning of 1966 are unknown but it has gone down on record that Holden Pitt, the company secretary of the sales company had been watching the sales figures and comparing them with expenditure. Certainly on 17 April 1967 he wrote a memorandum to Lord at the Harley Street office:

'The increase in sales in 1966 of approximately 10,000 sq yd a week with a higher offset content has not been sufficient to support the capital investment programme and the heavy overhead cost relating thereto. No contribution has, therefore, resulted and in this current year (to 31 May 1967) with sales slightly under the 1966 level, the effect is more pronounced.'

There are no visible signs that this warning influenced Lord very much for on 12 May 1967 he paid £150,000 for the Kyle chain of paint and wallpaper shops which at that time were making a loss. True, the payments were to be spread over five years but it was nevertheless not a transaction one might have expected from a company which already had its own considerable problems. Nor were the shops very suitable for carpet sales because some of them were so small that they couldn't give the space for Lord's products to be unrolled; others were in very second class shopping positions.

Lord's idea was to buy the shops as a tax loss situation,

restore them to profitability—he believed this would be possible by selling only four or five carpets a week in each shop—and then to set the past losses of the shops against the profits of the carpet business. But in fact no more than 2% of Lord's output was ever sold through the shops and they lost about £126,000 in a single year.

This move also antagonised Lord's salesmen who now felt that their fight, at a difficult time, was made even more uphill. They not only had the competition against them but their own shops were trying to grab sales. It is worth remembering that Lord's salesmen were not ordinary full-time paid men who, although they might grouse were still drawing a salary each week. The success of the entire Lord operation depended to an enormous extent on the keenness of his 2,000 teachers, local government officials—even clergymen—who were part-time agents. They were backed by only 150 full-time representatives who could never hope alone to secure the volume required to keep the empire ticking over, let alone expand it.

In addition to all his other problems Lord had to face the fact (but failed to do so) that by the spring of 1967 the carpet market was beginning to change. Nearly 10 years before Lord had confounded his competitors by using a new method of carpet manufacture and exploiting the economic and technical advantages by dynamic and unusual marketing. Now the competitors were coming back, exploiting a shift in public taste away from the flat 'unsculptured' carpets by Lord towards the more elaborate Axminster-type designs. In other words patterns were in again. Another factor which was working against Lord was that with his factory sited in Northern Ireland it took him up to six or seven weeks to deliver an order; when his carpets were a novelty both in texture and price this did not matter very much but as the competition strengthened, and he was undercut on price, the better deliveries offered by the home manufacturers often clinched the deal.

Lord made one attempt to challenge the opposition by launching a 'sculptured' carpet of his own, to be known as Chunky. He conceived this idea in the winter of 1966 and once again it was the old Lord story. Convinced he was right it was, as one executive put it, 'all rush, rush, rush'. Once again the market research was omitted, the technical abilities of the product insufficiently tested.

When the carpets were marketed it proved to be disastrous. The unusually long fibre needed to give the carpet its sculptured effect did not spring back as it should when trodden on. So many complaints poured in that three weeks after the launch the company was compelled to offer to take every single carpet back again and to refund the customers' money. These carpets, designed to sell on the home market at 55/6d a square yard were eventually sold abroad for 17/6d.

Because of competition Lord now found himself in the Bloom situation so far as his advertising was concerned. In 1966/7 he spent £150,000 more in advertising for slightly fewer sales. Like Bloom he began to buy sales at an uneconomically high cost.

This huge advertising expenditure pushed customers into his expensively sited shops but now the salesmen began to find that they were treating them as ordinary carpet shops and asking to see a range—something which was just not available in the Lord outlets. These shops were a very heavy overhead for the company. Their numbers had nearly doubled over the past three years and some of them attracted rents of £10,000 a year. There were 90 in all, yet between them they were only responsible for about 30% of the turnover. They had probably been running at a loss longer than Lord or anyone else in the company realised.

In 1966, the happy record year, the turnover was £10.8 million and the profit £1.3 million. In 1967 turnover was down to £10.3 million but profits had dropped disastrously, as we have seen. In 1968 the turnover had dropped by another £300,000 but now the profit was not only down, it had disappeared altogether and turned into a thumping great loss of £556,000. Thus although sales declined by only £½ million over three years the company suffered a profit drain of no less than £1.8 million.

These figures were bad enough but they were tragic and disastrous when placed against Lord's and MacMillan's forecasts on which, presumably, the vast expenditure was based. In 1967 profits of £875,000 for the full year had been forecast, whereas £458,000 only had been achieved. In 1968 they forecast a profit of £1.1 million and ended up with a loss of £556,000. It is astonishing—and perhaps explains these miscalculations—that right up until the end the company had no full-time financial controller. The situation was not helped by the fact that the Lord empire, the House of Lord, was in fact two separate entities: Cyril Lord Carpets Ltd and Cyril Lord Carpet Sales Ltd. Each had its own managing director and thus the absence of comment from the executives around Lord as things went from bad to worse becomes more understandable—half the time they just did not know the real situation. There was, however, no sinister reason for the division of these two companies. They had not been created on the basis that 'divided I rule'; taxation was the main reason for the arrangement, bearing in mind that purchase tax is involved in carpets. Lord found it most convenient for the production company to sell its products to the sales company at or very near cost; thus the sales company took all the profits, a perfectly legitimate arrangement, but one which impeded communication between the two companies.

When the crisis became apparent Lord reacted characteristically; always a hard worker, he started a 22-hour a day regimen. But it was too little and too late and, harrassed not only in business but in his personal life (his son, Peter, had a very serious car accident in November) Lord, now in his midfifties had a blackout on 1 July 1967, falling unconscious to the floor and cutting his head. The doctors diagnosed high blood pressure, warned him off fatty foods and told him that if he wanted to live he must take as much rest as possible.

Lord took their advice and entered a clinic for treatment for the whole of July. At the end of August he went to the West Indies for a holiday but in September flew to Montreal for a visit to Expo '67. He returned in October to present the company's disastrous loss of £556,000 but was away again in November due to illness.

It was not characteristic of Lord, however unwell, to give up at this point and it seems likely that he failed to realise the real nature of the crisis which his company was facing. The prices of the carpets were raised and advertising was cut back but otherwise very little was done. Commenting, Stephen Aris and Brian Moynihan said of this time 'Lord and his top executives carried on seemingly oblivious that the company was bleeding to death.' Nevertheless in September of 1967 Lord and McMillan cut their salaries by 50% and waived dividends amounting to £36,872. But this saving, in the order of a total of £50,000, was only a drop in the ocean, because sales were now falling off so fast.

By December rumours were circulating pretty generally in the City and in two weeks the share price dropped from 11/- to 7/9d and it was rumoured that Capital Finance, the Edin- burgh hire purchase company which had been discounting a large part of Lord's hire purchase business, had some £3 million worth of bad debts. This particular rumour was in fact a lying jade : Lord had never had too much trouble from defaulting customers although the administration of the hire purchase business which the company handled itself was administratively very costly. At this stage the company's troubles were classic : it had spent too much and had sold too little; it was acutely short of working capital.

Reluctantly Lord agreed to raise cash by selling off some of the expensive and unprofitable showrooms. It was finally agreed to get rid of all the showrooms and replace them with 800 agents, but to do it discreetly so that they did not flood the market and go below their market price. The idea went sour. All the shops were placed in the hands of an agent with strict instructions to make their own selection and then stagger the sales. But the existence of the complete list leaked out and word that all the shops were for sale damaged not only the market prices but the company too.

About this time Lord realised that he would have to leave

and that he was physically incapable of carrying on. His doctors were stressing the danger of a heart attack if he continued to worry about the business. Still he hesitated to make a final decision. At the end of December 1967 he left for another holiday—this time to Madeira—and when he came back in the middle of January 1968 he finally agreed to leave. Before doing so he approached Eric Crabtree, an old friend who was then chairman of Hardie Amies, asking whether he would take over the Chairmanship. These negotiations broke down and William McMillan took over.

Lord set off for the Bahamas and while he was there his shares, then worth some £400,000 were transferred from London via an investment company called Far East Nominees.

On 4 April his resignation was officially announced and for the next nine months McMillan and his assistant Dennis Wood, struggled desperately to save the company. Several merchant banks were approached for help. Rothschilds declined but Hill Samuel accepted. A detailed report on the company's financial position was prepared; a financial controller was approached and 168 employees were declared redundant.

McMillan and Wood also put in hand some drastic steps. The majority of the standard carpet lines were stopped and an entirely new range was planned for the Autumn. The Kyle shop deal was unscrambled and Cyrilawn was sold abroad. There was also a carpet sale in August 1968 to get rid of £1 million of stocks which had built up as sales had lagged. The personality cult was also discounted and Cyril Lord Carpet Sales Ltd became Rathgael Carpets Ltd. The company staggered on until November 1968 when Viyella took over its assets for only £2 million.

The Cost of Price-Cutting

Rolls Razor
1958-1964

O NE of the most spectacular business failures since the war has been the fall of John Bloom's Rolls Razor washing machine empire—a venture which, by selling cheaply direct to the housewife, forced other manufacturers to think hard and long about their own prices. In fact Rolls Razor did a great deal to make the washing machine commonplace in virtually every home in Britain.

For John Bloom, son of an East End tailor, it all started early in 1958. At that time he was operating a paraffin tanker, selling mostly to West Indians in London. Then an Irishman, Mick Cosgrave, introduced him to the idea of buying cheap washing machines from Holland for around £29 each and selling them door-to-door for about £50. The foundation of this business was the credit sale where the customer pays only a low deposit but at that time was required to settle the balance in nine months. After a successful trial run Bloom set himself up in a tiny office in North London, calling his company the North London Advertising and Distributing Company and using Belmont Finance Corporation to fund his sales. He soon hired a couple of salesmen on a commission-only basis and advertised his machine by door-to-door circulars.

For a few months the business prospered but then the North

London Advertising and Distributing Company was in trouble because customers were defaulting on their payments and Belmont Finance Corporation naturally made recourse to Bloom and his partner.

Bloom decided to go over to hire purchase sales with the far smaller monthly repayments and a bigger deposit. He knew that this would make his customers think more carefully whether they could afford the machine but he needed an even cheaper model. He finally located a satisfactory twin-tub—a washer and spin drier combined—at a factory just outside Utrecht and arranged to have his stock flown in through Channel Air Bridge, which at that time operated from Southend. The new machine was more expensive, not cheaper.

Soon the firm's name was changed to Continental Washing Machine Company and it moved into bigger offices in Old Street. Bloom stopped cold canvassing and instead advertised in the press.

The first advertisement was in the *Evening News*—for the 'Klean' machine which cost the company about £52 and which they offered at £108 with an allowance of up to £35 in part exchange for old boilers or washing machines. This allowance was a way round the compulsory hire purchase deposit which at that time was nearly 40%. On a £108 machine this meant that the housewife should have put down £40 but if she got £35 in part exchange she only had to find another £5. The Continental Washing Machine Company was thus selling the Klean for £73, a profit of £21. Unfortunately for Bloom the Board of Trade stepped in fairly promptly on the grounds that the allowance was being used as a means to contravene the hire purchase regulations.

Bloom set off again to find a twin-tub which he could buy for about £30 and sell for between £40 and £50—less than half the price of most washing machines then on the market. His search led him to the Schrouten Brothers who had just started making a twin-tub which they were prepared to sell to Bloom for £23. This machine Bloom named the 'Electromatic' and early in the next year the name of the company was changed to the Electromatic Washing Machine Company.

In Britain he started to sell the Electromatic in two versions, one for 49 guineas and the other, a de luxe model with a heater, for 59 guineas. Convinced that he was at last on to a winner he borrowed £1,000 from his uncle and took a back page of the *Daily Mirror* which at that time cost £424. This advertisement drew 8,000 enquiries and was the beginning of the revolution. When people saw the price of the Electromatic they suddenly realised that a washing machine was no longer a luxury.

Bloom immediately had a cash flow problem because the Schroutens, asked to turn out 100 machines a week, wanted substantial advances to finance production. Bloom kept afloat by selling the Electromatics quickly, using the money from the hire purchase companies to pay the Schroutens, and taking longer credit from Channel Air Bridge.

Within a few weeks the company had four regional depots each serving area salesmen and the Schroutens's production capacity of 100 machines a week was soon exceeded. Bloom took off again for Europe to find additional manufacturers.

The troubles of success soon began to pile up. Desperate for more supplies he went to Italy and imported a few hundred of the 'Jetmatic' but they did not wash very thoroughly and proved a financial disaster. The premises at Old Street were also quite unsuitable for the large volume of business he was now doing and he was forced to move to Great Eastern Street. Then Channel Air Bridge began to press them hard for the £11,300 which they owed. Bloom talked convincingly to Freddy Laker, the proprietor, and Laker agreed to accept £1,000 a fortnight until the debt was cleared.

Still desperate for cash Bloom seized on a clause in the purchase tax regulations which said that if washing machines were assembled or even part-assembled in Britain purchase tax was payable only every four months, instead of having to pay it as soon as they were imported. This meant that Bloom would get a credit of £2,000 a week and over four months could use more than £30,000 to fund the whole Electromatic operation. He decided that the simplest way of doing this would be to put motors in an otherwise complete machine and thus he started buying from Hoover, and also started his career as a manufacturer of washing machines.

Once again the company moved, this time to Romford in Essex.

In 1959 Bloom met Louis Jackson, a financier who introduced him to Colin Kingham and Arthur Sowley, Chairman and Secretary of Rolls Razor Ltd. Bloom was seeking a merger with an old-established public company which was short of money, or looking for something to replace a traditional product that had lost its selling power. The attraction for Bloom was that if he went 'public' he could enhance his personal fortune and the business would enjoy the tax advantages of a public company.

Rolls Razor Ltd had been established in the late 20's and before the war had established themselves with an unattractive-looking but economical ever-lasting razor, a sort of compromise between the cut-throat and the safety razor. However by 1959, badly hit by the introduction of the electric razor, production was down to about 1,000 razors a week and to keep the staff in employment Rolls was largely on contract work, making rifle magazines and pull-throughs. Accumulated losses until 1960, over four years, proved to be £115,000.

Rolls themselves had been involved in the design of a washing machine in an attempt to diversify their business. It was called the 'Rolls-a-Matic' and operated on a vibratory system. In Bloom's opinion, however it was not a viable proposition but Rolls had the equipment and the tool-room staff to make any type of washing machine or part that he wanted. They also had excellent premises at Cricklewood in North London.

The deal was clinched promptly. It was arranged that Bloom should become Managing Director of Rolls Razor and that Rolls would start assembling washing machines for Electromatic, in the main still using parts supplied by the Schroutens, who by that time had expanded production to keep pace with sales, but also using several components made at Cricklewood. The financial arrangements were somewhat more complicated. Jackson introduced Bloom to Gilbert Southall whose plan was that Equity and Share Company (London) Ltd, in which he had a considerable interest, would bid for all three million Rolls' shares and that providing Bloom agreed to sell Electromatic to Rolls at a later date 1,180,000 of the Rolls shares were to be transferred to Bloom at the price Southall paid for them.

On 19 November 1959 Southall's Equity and Share made their bid, operating through another firm, Harley Street Securities, offering one shilling for every Rolls share, which were then standing at $4\frac{1}{2}$d each. It had already been arranged that the directors would accept immediately which gave Southall 21% of the shareholding and soon he held 60%. By the end of the year the price of the shares had shot up to around six shillings each. The Stock Exchange, who demand that a share price should be a true reflection of a company's prosperity, were suspicious and they suspended dealings in the shares on 8 January 1960. The shares were then standing at seven shillings and had been as high as 7s $2\frac{1}{2}$d earlier.

Louis Jackson also persuaded Bloom to sign an agreement which gave Jackson a large percentage of any shares that Bloom received and 5% of his future earnings. This agreement proved costly for Bloom—to the tune of £330,000 when Jackson's executors started a legal action against him in 1964.

At the same time Bloom also signed another agreement, this time for the eventual sale of Electromatic to Rolls, in return for which he would receive three million shares in Rolls.

The first advertisement for the Rolls Electromatic washing machine appeared on 13 January 1960 and was the start of a £200,000 national advertising campaign.

In the new company Gilbert Southall was Chairman and Mark Horowitz (his solicitor) was a director to look after the interests of Equity and Share. Bloom became a director in February and was appointed Managing Director in March.

Almost immediately the new Rolls organisation was faced with a dangerous situation. Jim Elvins, one of Bloom's associates, started his own company with the help of the Schroutens —another direct-selling operation for washing machines, this time the 'Duomatic'. This company took a good half of Bloom's salesmen and managers but worst still the Schrouten Brothers now refused to supply Bloom with machines, so that within two weeks Rolls were completely out of stock. Customers had to be told there would be an eight-week delay in delivery. Bloom, nothing daunted, started at short notice the tremendous task of setting up a complete production line at Cricklewood. But the first machines off the line were, as Bloom himself has admitted, inferior and there were soon complaints to the press. Also many customers who had waited weeks for a machine after paying their deposit were starting to get restive. The Newspaper Proprietors Association demanded a visit to Cricklewood so that they could decide whether Rolls should be allowed to continue advertising in national newspapers.

Bloom immediately started an operation to convince them that Rolls was producing a large number of machines. When the representatives of the NPA arrived everyone available was bent over a piece of machinery or metal, secondhand machines were busily being taken apart and put together again and, the production of the previous week having been held back, it was possible to show an impressive number of washing machines awaiting delivery. Happy that production was in full swing Rolls was allowed to continue advertising.

Throughout the whole of that summer Rolls was beset with production problems. First there was trouble with the spin-drier brake; then the special pump which Bloom had introduced for emptying the dirty water direct into the sink was unsatisfactory and housewives all over the country wrote complaining that their kitchens had been flooded. Anxious about the knocking the name Electromatic was getting the next modification was advertised as the Starmatic but these suffered an even worse fate because the motors, imported from Germany, blew up at the second or third usage by the housewife.

I

By June 1960 production had reached 500 a week but, in spite of all the complaints, Rolls were still not keeping up with the demand. To all who complained a replacement machine was supplied and if any clothing was damaged the company paid the bills. This policy paid off and, in spite of some of the early disastrous engineering problems, confidence spread throughout the country and laid the foundations for the later tremendous build-up of sales.

In October 1960 the Rolls 66 was introduced with a motor which operated both the washer and the drier and this was the first of their successful models. At the same time Bloom came to an agreement with Rolls giving him an option to buy Electromatic and he bought the 1,180,000 shares that had been promised by Gilbert Southall. To do this he borrowed money from Leadenhall Sterling Investments. It was first arranged that Leadenhall should lend the company £165,000 but before they would do this they wanted to hold as security the shares Bloom had agreed to buy from Southall. In order to buy them Leadenhall lent Bloom £60,000 which he paid back in 1961. Thus although Leadenhall were holding them the purchase of these shares made Bloom the largest single shareholder in Rolls with 58% of the equity.

For 1960 Bloom had planned on a profit of £30,000; as the year drew to a close his accountants forecast a loss of over £200,000, mainly due to the disastrous machines.

The razor-making side of the business, which had continued, was also losing a considerable amount of money and they were actively looking around for diversification. The first venture was not a great success: because Rolls had a traditional market for the razors in the chemist shops they introduced an artificial sun-tan, Man-Tan which did not, however, prove financially viable.

But during 1961 sales of washing machines climbed to 68,000—more than double the 29,000 of 1960—and Rolls was considerably restructured.

Richard Reader Harris, who was then Conservative Member for Heston and Isleworth and Billy Rees-Davies, then

Conservative Member for the Isle of Thanet, joined the Board. By now Bloom had acquired a very considerable experience of selling washing machines but was still light in matters of finance and the ways of the City. Reader Harris became Chairman of Rolls in July 1961 and provided Bloom with many financial contacts. Fenn and Crosthwaite were appointed the Company's stock brokers and Price Waterhouse the auditors. Kleinworts agreed to take charge of refloating the company on the Stock Exchange, following a detailed investigation into its affairs.

About this time Bloom met Sir Charles Colston who had been the brains behind the success of Hoover in Britain. He retired from Hoover in 1954 after 30 years as Managing Director and had begun his own business, Charles Colston Ltd, which was making dishwashers. At this stage they were costing not far short of £100 and were considered a luxury—as indeed they are still to a large extent—and while the Rolls-Colston was to put dishwashers on the map in Britain Bloom never achieved quite the same breakthrough as he did with washing machines.

Colston came on to the Rolls board and it was agreed that a joint company should be set up to handle dishwashers. Rolls bought Sir Charles's factory at High Wycombe and at the end of 1961 began selling direct to the housewife. The first model cost only 49 guineas with a de luxe model at 66 guineas. The Board of the associated company had Sir Charles as chairman and joint managing director with Bloom and Reader Harris as deputy chairman. Henry Oppenheim, chairman of City Wall Properties; Michael Colston, son of Sir Charles; and Aaron Wright, a close associate of Sir Charles, were the other directors. Another advantage of this connection was that Sir Charles was also a director of Tallent Engineering in County Durham and their production capacity was turned over to making washing machines for Rolls. At this point Bloom sold 50,000 of his own shares in Rolls to Oppenheim for 8s 9d each.

In December 1961 Rolls finally agreed to buy Electromatic

I*

from Bloom. This had been agreed in principle during the takeover of January 1960, when Rolls were going to issue Bloom with three million shares in return for Electromatic, providing that Electromatic's net assets at the end of the year were £150,000 or more and that the Stock Exchange restored dealings in Rolls shares. However, the Committee on Quotations had refused to requote the shares and since a quotation seemed unlikely for some time the original Rolls-Electromatic agreement had been scrapped.

A later agreement made in October 1960 provided Rolls with an option to buy Electromatic whether the quotation was restored or not. This time Bloom was to be given two million shares providing Electromatic had net assets of £100,000. When the audit for 1961 was completed Price Waterhouse were able to report assets of £108,403 and it was thus agreed to buy Electromatic on 1 January 1962. The shares Bloom received were worth perhaps £1 million and with the shares he had received from Gilbert Southall he was worth around £2 million, but only on paper until a Stock Exchange quotation was restored. Nevertheless, this deal made him the majority shareholder in Rolls with 64% and he was now sitting on a very comfortable commercial property. In the first nine months of 1961 Rolls and Electromatic made around £280,000.

Although Rolls was now set fair for 1962 and it looked as though they would once again get a Stock Exchange quotation vested interests were moving against them. They were criticised in the House of Commons during a debate on a private member's Hire Purchase Bill, intended to stamp out unscrupulous high pressure door-to-door selling and switch-selling. It was reported in the House that Rolls's washing machines had attracted 'a quite unprecedentedly large number of complaints from dissatisfied customers'. It was alleged that the Consumers Advisory Council had stated that of 400 members with Rolls machines as many as 50 had made complaints and that a national newspaper advertising the machines had received 250 complaints. Reader Harris replied for the company stating that it had 150,000 hire purchase customers and thus the percentage was small. The *Daily Mirror* was the newspaper involved and had in fact received 256 complaints, but these were over a period of four years and were mainly in connection with late deliveries.

In 1962 Rolls started a new venture : the establishment of shops selling goods at less than the manufacturers' recommended prices in an attempt to kill off retail price maintenance, which was in many areas already on its last legs. But this was not so in the home appliances field and Rolls immediately aroused the antagonism of most manufacturers, some of whom cut off supplies. The first shop in the projected Rolls Discount Store Group opened early in 1962 in East Ham. As well as Rolls products it featured Hotpoint washing machines, Berry fires, Morphy-Richards irons, Bulpit kettles, Pifco hair driers, and electric blankets, all with at least 15% off the list price.

The shop was an immediate success and others soon followed at Cricklewood, Southend, Wood Green, Portsmouth, Nottingham and Bristol. But the manufacturers did not let much grass grow under their feet and within a few weeks Morphy-Richards had obtained a High Court injunction to stop the sale of any of their goods at a cut price. This was a bitter blow although the shops struggled on for some time before closing. They were two years too early (resale price maintenance was abolished in 1964).

Brighter news in that spring of 1962 was that the Stock Exchange had agreed that Rolls shares could be quoted again and Kleinworts decided to fix the price of the requoted shares by offering 500,000 of them for sale by tender at a minimum price of £1. The tender system means that people can offer any sum they like with a 'reserve' of £1 for each share and that the 500,000 are then distributed amongst the highest bidders. The price at which the shares are subsequently quoted when they go onto the market is the lowest figure at which any single share of the 50,000 were sold. The official price of Rolls's shares thus started at 23 shillings. Bloom's own holding became worth about £3.5 million—officially.

By the middle of 1962 Rolls were selling 2,500 washing machines a week and were once again in production diffi-cuties. Cricklewood was going flat out but unable to cope. Bloom found that the Pressed Steel Company had a factory in South Wales producing Prestcold refrigerators at about a quarter of its total capacity. The £5 million plant, built only two years earlier, covered some 50 acres and Bloom was delighted to find that Pressed Steel could make an identical machine to the one manufactured in Cricklewood for only £23, £6 less than in London. Badly hit by the motor industry recession (Pressed Steel also made bodies for the car industry) they further agreed that Rolls could market their Prestcold refrigerator by direct selling.

Thus on 9 September 1962 Pressed Steel and Rolls ex-changed shares worth about £750,000. Pressed Steel took up 500,000 Rolls shares which gave them a 10% interest in that company and Rolls took up over 900,000 or about 3½% of the Pressed Steel shares. Production at the Cricklewood factory was run down and the factory space largely converted into a warehouse, although a few people were kept on making the razors. South Wales was overjoyed but the decision to close down Cricklewood attracted quite a lot of adverse publicity for Rolls. It led also to the resignation of Sir Charles Colston from the Rolls Board. He was anxious to develop Rolls production at Tallent Engineering and considered, rightly, that Pressed Steel, with its much larger and more modern factory, was a serious competitor.

Following the Pressed Steel deal Bloom made one of his characteristic moves: he slashed anything from £10 to £30 off Prestcold prices—as indeed he could afford to do since he was now going to sell direct. This swift action aroused tremendous hostility in the electrical retailing field when shop-keepers all over the country found themselves lumbered with old stock that they must sell at a reduced profit or even a loss.

By the end of 1962 Rolls and its ebullient managing director could fairly claim to be the most hated company

and industrialist in the country. Both manufacturers and retailers of domestic appliances were up in arms. An orgy of
price-cutting, anti-Rolls newspaper advertisements and City
rumours followed. But, as Bloom has said proudly, the immediate effect was nil; by the end of 1962 Rolls had sold
101,000 washing machines and had cornered 12% of the
market. His profit for that year was £720,000, on which
Rolls paid a 100% dividend. Bloom had certainly won a
series of major battles but, a year later, came his Waterloo and
he had lost a war.

During 1962, the advertising campaign personally directed
by Bloom kept going at full blast ('You are going to read the
most astonishing advertisement ever' was one of his less
dramatic headlines). The whole organisation had spent a
good deal of time and money in the development of an automatic washing machine and late in 1962 a prototype was
developed. Unfortunately his chief designer, Irving Jacobs,
announced that he had worked out the idea for the suspension
system, which made the machine both small and cheap, in
his own time; he had patented the idea personally and thus
Rolls, he said, could not be allowed to make the automatic
except under licence. Rolls had no alternative but to agree
but in fact the automatic never got off the ground. At the
time of the liquidation there were only three prototypes in
existence because of various technical problems.

In 1961 Bloom had met Sir Isaac Wolfson and a close, if
informal relationship had been established between the two
men. Bloom certainly consulted Wolfson before finalising
many of his deals and observers at the time said that there
was an almost father-son relationship. Wolfson is known to
have been tremendously impressed by the Pressed Steel-
Prestcold deal and at one time it looked as though Drages, his
finance company, would make a bid for Rolls at around 33
shillings a share. Bloom agreed in principle, the news got
around and the share price rose in anticipation but by then
Bloom's name was involved in the Blue Gardenia Club murder
trial and, understandably, Sir Isaac preferred to let the dust

settle before proceeding with the takeover. In fact it never occurred but it is interesting to speculate whether Rolls might not still be with us today if Wolfson had taken it in hand.

Undoubtedly the Blue Gardenia Club murder trial did both Bloom and Rolls a good deal of harm. In brief, Harvey Holford, owner of the Blue Gardenia night club in Brighton was arrested towards the end of 1962 and charged with the murder of his wife Christine. He pleaded not guilty but at Sussex Assizes in the spring of 1963 he was sentenced to three years imprisonment for manslaughter on the grounds of provocation and diminished responsibility. The basis of the defence was that Holford had been driven to it because his wife, who had spent some time in the South of France the previous summer had been playing around with men and flaunting her conquests in front of her husband. One man so flaunted was supposed to be Bloom.

Even before the case came on Holford took out a writ against Bloom claiming that he had enticed his late wife away from him and so the headlines proclaimed 'Man on murder charge sues millionaire Bloom for enticement'. Bloom was never called at the trial and thus he had no chance of refuting these allegations, although following the Rolls crash he did so most vigorously in his book 'It's no Sin to Make a Profit'.

In 1963 more diversification came about with the acquisition of Bylock, a company which had been making motors for Rolls since the previous year. The firm had begun as makers of various electrical appliances but when they went public in 1947 they concentrated on vacuum cleaners. A credit squeeze had however forced them to diversify again and in the autumn of 1962 they were making washing machines, floor polishers, hair driers, automatic irons, food mixers and fan heaters. They were losing about £70,000 a year and had not paid a dividend since 1959.

Almost half the voting shares were controlled by the four directors, Bertrand Latham, Cecil Mathes and his father, and L. W. Moscrop.

At this time Rolls were concerned about the effects of their Pressed Steel deal on AEI and Hoover, who were also producing their wash tub motors. They believed that possibly these two companies might freeze their supplies and that production would be jeopardised. If they took over Bylock, they reasoned, they would get a fool-proof supply for their motors. Rolls offered one of their shares for every 15 Bylock shares. With the directors and their families agreeing Rolls had 45½% of the shares tied up, including 3% which they already owned. They speedily acquired the majority.

However, this was not sufficient because the Rolls plan was to break up the firm, selling off the assets, maintaining its service division, and transferring the motor making section to Pressed Steel's Swansea plant. By company law they had to have 100% control although there is a clause in the provision which says that if a bidder obtains 90% of the shares he may make a forced purchase of the other 10%.

Bloom has always considered Bylock one of his great mistakes and has always stated that he never intended to make the offer unconditional unless he had the 90%. But at a critical stage in negotiations he took off for America and in his absence some confusion arose.

By 31 March 1963 Rolls had got 71.3% of the ordinary shares and 35% of the 'A' shares and in Bloom's absence the offer had been made unconditional. Rolls now had a company which they could not break up in the way Bloom had planned. In this situation Bloom saw a possible plot to take over his power within the Rolls empire and immediately he returned to England he reorganised the main board of Rolls, appointing his two brothers-in-law as directors.

The Bylock deal also brought into the open the long standing feud between Bloom and Jack Jacobs, who had been deputy managing director. He was asked to stand down and on 18 April 1963 Bloom issued a memorandum stating that he was chief executive of the company and that all departmental heads were responsible to the Board through him, that he was in charge of the company's policies and that Reader

Harris was in charge of all contracts with Kleinwort, the company's brokers, and other City institutions.

The Bylock situation continued to cause concern at Rolls. At the annual meeting in 1963 Reader Harris, as the new chairman, announced that the firm had lost £175,000 in the year to July 1962 and that the bank was pressing hard for repayment of the £155,000 overdraft.

Bylock had one piece of property which Rolls thought was of value, the Lewyt vacuum cleaner which was built on an unusual principle. It had two motors, one at the end of a flexible hose and the other in its cylinder, which gave it the flexibility of cylinder models and the powerful suction of traditional cleaners. It was agreed to make a smaller version of the standard model which could be sold to Rolls for £4 and which should be given away with the washing machines to help boost sales. These little cleaners were the first of the Rolls free gifts or premium offers. They were phenomenally successful and troubles almost imediately ensued because Bylock had a production capacity of only 1,000 a week whereas at that time Rolls were selling something like 4,000 washing machines. Within three weeks of the initial advertising campaign Rolls were 9,000 behind in deliveries and other premiums were frantically sought. It has been one of Bloom's contentions that premium offers caused so many administrative difficulties in Rolls that they were a principle reason for the failure of the company.

Meanwhile Rolls carried on their full scale campaign against the retailers. Advertisements in the national press pointed out that 'Up to 40% of the cost of most electrical goods on sale in British shops and stores is taken by the middle men. On a quality washing machine their profits can amount to more than £30.'

The Radio and Television Retailers Association were not slow to fight back and announced they had set up a fighting fund aimed at getting £100,000 to launch a campaign against Rolls. The trade magazine *Electrical and Retail Trading* threw in their support and the Appliance Trade Association was formed and launched another fighting fund. Hoover, Hotpoint, Parnall, Servis, English Electric and Electrolux threw themselves into the fray.

But on the whole the counterblast was a failure. Committee rule was no match for Bloom, although it is possible that this opposition led Rolls to wilder and wilder premium fantasies. Certainly Rolls shares, which had stood at 35 shillings at the time of the Prestcold price cuts were down to 22 shillings by the end of October 1963 although it is more than likely that sharp observers in the City were already beginning to detect the cracks in the impressive Rolls facade. In fact these were so serious that their brokers Fenn and Crosthwaite issued 'an authoritative denial of all the adverse rumours affecting Rolls Razor'.

The statement said: 'A number of rumours regarding Rolls Razor, its method of trading, the quality of its products, its ability to meet its accounts and its general solvency have been circulated. These rumours have reached considerable proportions and there has been some nervous selling which the Cuban crisis brought to a climax. Although it has nothing to do with Rolls Razor as an operating company, the fact that Mr John Bloom, the Managing Director, has been mentioned in a recent court case and widely headlined may also have had its effect.

'We are glad to be able to tell our clients that the Chairman of Rolls Razor, the Chairman of Pressed Steel and the Chairman of Drages authorise us to say that Rolls Razor has operated and is operating successfully, that it is entirely solvent, that all its creditors are being and have been paid in the normal way and that all its salesmen are and always have been, expressly forbidden to attempt "switch selling".'

One immediate effect of the anti-Rolls campaign was that existing machines sold through the shops were reduced considerably and new models were introduced at much lower prices. Rolls forced English Electric, Hotpoint and Hoover to slash prices and overseas competition was not slow to take advantage of the collapse of the market. Philips and a number of Italian firms came in swiftly and Great Universal Stores promoted the Acme Challenge to be sold by mail order, through the retail outlets in the group and by the GUS salesmen collectors.

This latest move aroused considerable speculation in the *Financial Times* and other papers as to why Sir Isaac Wolfson, as chairman of GUS was launching an attack on Rolls while, as chairman of Drages he was supplying the company with £10 million of hire purchase finance. The answer, of course, was that GUS had independent marketing policies.

Nevertheless, in spite of this opposition Rolls's sales forged ahead and on 7 November 1962 they forecast a 100% dividend for the year instead of the 80% predicted previously. In January 1963 sales topped 3,000 a week for the first time ever.

Nevertheless the City was not happy and Rolls shares were unsteady. In February 1963 Bloom proposed that they should announce a dividend for that year of 200%, double the prediction for 1962. Bloom planned to double the number of washing machines sold during 1963 over the previous year and in this he succeeded by selling 201,400 by the end of December.

It was also agreed it would be useful for Rolls to have support in America on Hoover's home ground. A quarter of a million shares were sold to the Investors Diversified Services, the biggest of the American mutual funds, who proposed holding the shares as a long term investment. Arrangements were also made for Rolls shares to be quoted on the New York Exchange.

During 1963 an extremely attractive Rolls offer was a washing machine and 3 cu ft capacity Prestcold refrigerator for only 59 guineas. But Rolls was losing about £5 on each Prestcold refrigerator. In addition the Bylock vacuum cleaner was eating into the washing machine profit margin.

Something was going wrong with Rolls's financial control because it was not until much later that the company came to realise that their basic washing machine, costing the housewife 39 guineas, was in fact being sold at a loss. And as washing machine prices went down throughout the market Rolls were selling more and more of the basic models. Bloom has said himself that in 1962 five out of every 100 machines were basics but in 1963 14 out of every 100 were in this category. Hire purchase debts were piling up, too, as they delved further into the lower income bracket.

At this period Rolls went mad. In 1963 Bloom announced that in the year ahead he would be spending about £2 million by putting an advertisement once a week in every national daily newspaper and in every Sunday paper each Sunday. Right at the beginning of the year Rolls signed a contract with the *News of the World* for £238,000, the biggest single advertising order ever placed with a national newspaper at that time. Bloom was one of the first people to use the editorial style advertisement in a large way and led to the newspapers insisting that 'Advertisers' Announcement' must appear at the head of every advertisement. Throughout the whole of Rolls history the advertising policy was Bloom's particular baby and he wrote many of the company's hard hitting advertisements.

Another venture of Bloom's during the summer of 1963 did not come off quite as he had planned. It centred on English and Overseas Investments who in 1961, through one of their subsidiaries, had backed a Rolls sales venture in Northern Ireland. At this time Bloom took an option to buy 100,000 English and Overseas two shilling shares for four shillings, an option which he took up in August 1962. In 1963 he suggested that English and Overseas should buy two companies which were connected with Rolls and in which Bloom had a personal interest. These were the Slough Die Casting Company, which made castings for Rolls and in which Bloom had a 55% interest; the other was Mercon Metals, who were also suppliers of Rolls. He then took up an option to buy 55% of the latter's shares in May 1963 and sold the two companies for 217,000 shares in English and Overseas. It was agreed that he would receive more shares, up to a maximum of one million, over the following three years and depending on the financial success of the two companies. Eventually, it was envisaged that Bloom would have a 40% stake in English and Overseas.

Bloom was interested in English and Overseas, a hire purchase firm, because it might serve him as his personal investment company in the same way as Sir Isaac Wolfson had Drages. It was proposed to him that he could buy English and Overseas shares with Rolls shares so that he held the English and Overseas shares and that the Rolls shares became English and Overseas' main asset. This would mean that the dividend on the Rolls holding would flow into English and Overseas where he would leave it to finance new projects.

The takeover was in fact accomplished and Sir Isaac Wolfson then suggested that not only should English and Overseas assume control of Rolls by taking over Bloom's shares but that Wolfson and Bloom should form a joint company to control English and Overseas.

Under this plan Bloom would receive something like a million English and Overseas shares and £1,135,000 convertible loan notes in return for his Rolls's shares. Secondly Drages would buy £1 million of English and Overseas loan notes from Bloom and finally Bloom would transfer 925,000 shares to a holding company in return for 50 shares of £1 in that company. Drages would transfer an equivalent value £740,000 in loan notes in return for the other 50 holding company shares. This was all arranged in an agreement between Sir Isaac Wolfson and Bloom on 17 October and a joint company called City and Commercial Developments was formed to act as the holding company.

Unfortunately in September of that year the executors of Jackson, the man who had originally introduced Rolls Razor to Bloom, began an action for the return of 318,500 Rolls's shares which were claimed as belonging to Jackson's estate. The executors threatened to take out a High Court injunction preventing Bloom disposing of any Rolls shares until their action had been heard. So the scheme came to nothing.

In spite of mammoth sales of washing machines Bloom had other worries in 1963. The Rolls Colston sales situation deteriorated steadily and the cut price at which each machine was sold was losing the company money. In the summer the price went back to around £80 in an attempt to reduce losses, but the venture had cost Rolls £85,000. Sir Charles acquired the £125,000 half share in Rolls-Colston appliances for £40,000 and Sir Charles renamed the company Colston Appliances. Rolls and its personnel withdrew completely from the board and the association with Colston ceased except that Tallent Engineering continued to supply washing machines.

Not daunted by the gathering clouds Rolls decided, in the autumn of 1963, to challenge Hoover with a new floor-level fan heater which that company had recently introduced. Typically and provocatively the new product was christened the Rolls 3333.

At a press conference on 3 October 1963 Bloom announced that he would offer about 60,000 heaters free with Rolls washing machines. Since Hoover were selling their heaters in the shops for around 14 guineas the effect can easily be imagined, especially as the announcement was made in the middle of Hoover's annual sales conference week. This announcement even got the company on BBC News, bringing a flood of letters protesting about 'advertising' by the BBC.

As 1963 drew to a close Rolls decided to aim for sales of 8,000 washing machines a week during the following year and planned to step up advertising to £3 million. These figures were not achieved and on advertising alone the company was probably paying out over twice as much as was warranted by sales. But during those last hectic months of 1963 all was optimism. Trading stamps, mail order and television rentals were all being planned. A scheme was also in hand to market washing machines and refrigerators direct to the Common Market countries. Rolls Rentals was started with a capital of £10,000 and an offer was made for the Firth Cleveland retail shop division which comprised nearly 500 outlets including the Wolfe and Hollander stores, Stones and the Broad-

mead shops. The bid was for £10 million through English and
Overseas with Sir Isaac Wolfson putting up the money. But
Firth Cleveland turned them down.

A few days later the company's involvement in trading
stamps was announced and towards the end of November
1963 Bloom obtained controlling interest in the Super Yellow
Stamp Trading Company Ltd and an option on Sir Isaac
Wolfson's Golden Eagle Stamp Company. Always an inno-
vator, Bloom stated he would offer cash for trading stamps as
an alternative to goods. In return for one of his books, which
cost £32 to fill, he intended giving 10 shillings in cash, or
goods worth between £1 and £1.10.d. This compared with
goods worth between 15s 9d and 16s being offered by rivals.

This is how *Newsweek* announced the launch:

'The stamps, naturally, are Bloom's own, called Super
Golden. They were launched in more than 10,000 outlets this
month amid a storm of ballyhoo keynoted by a press conference at which Bloom's trading stamp manager appeared in a
gold suit and tie escorted by a gaggle of golden-haired
beauties. Characteristically, Bloom could think of no better
design for the stamps than his own face, and his churning
publicity mill quickly issued the grandiose claim that Supa
John's stamps were "the first in the world ever to have incorporated the head of an individual in its presentation other
than the King or Queen of England".'

Most of Bloom's diversifications came to nothing. Another
was his Bulgarian holiday venture—Eastern European holidays on a package basis. He proposed offering a fortnight's
holiday in Bulgaria to cost from 45 guineas by plane and 29
guineas by coach—highly competitive at the time, as indeed
were all ventures which Bloom contemplated. But he met all
sorts of technical difficulties which he failed to overcome
especially as he was forced to turn his attention to a break-
down in the production arrangement with Pressed Steel. Although personalities were involved the major problem was that

by the end of 1963 Pressed Steel said they could no longer afford to make a twin tub for only £23. No agreement was reached and Pressed Steel sold their Rolls holding and Rolls sold their Pressed Steel shares. Rolls lost about £40,000 on the transaction while Pressed Steel made a profit of about a quarter of a million on their Rolls shares. Sir Charles Colston rejoined the board of Rolls on the basis that Tallent Engineering might take over the whole of the Rolls production. Nearly 1,500 workers became redundant at Swansea as a result of the break.

Rolls handled their public relations in this matter badly and caused yet another crisis of confidence. The general situation was also deteriorating rapidly. In the first three months of 1964 the company sold 54,794 washing machines, a 21.5% share of the British market but this was only half of the sales planned and only half of production capacity and raw material supplies. In March sales began to decline still further, in spite of the enormous advertising budget. Premiums were also rapidly getting out of hand; at this time the company was giving away complete sets of kitchen tools, fan heaters, cutlery, crockery, high-fi radiograms and vacuum cleaners.

At the beginning of March 1964 all premium offers were stopped and the company concentrated on offering holidays and Supa Golden Stamps, with extra stamps for people who disposed of their second hand washing machines, of which the company now had an enormous stock. They also brought out a new machine called the Rolls Concord; *Which* did not help by commenting unfavourably on Rolls's hire purchase terms. The City was getting more and more jittery but many, less well informed, still saw Bloom as the golden boy of British finance, the gallant knight who had brought prices down for the housewife. Here is *Newsweek* on Bloom :

'For England's 32-year-old John Bloom, it's been one long, glorious romp. Pale, slight, sporting a fuzzy little beard to hide his youth, the non-U son of a London tailor appears ludicrously miscast as a captain of British industry. Yet in commerce as in politics, nothing is so powerful as an idea whose time has come. And the flamboyant Bloom had both the idea —slash prices on home appliances in high-margin Britain— and the brass to exploit it.

'Factories working for Bloom-controlled Rolls-Razor Ltd, last week turned out some 5,000 washer-driers and 2,000 refrigerators alone . . . Astonished Britons not only have been buying his washers and refrigerators, but are snapping up vacuum cleaners, heaters and a host of other appliances as fast as they are produced.

'Loudly championing the cause of the cut rate . . . the exuberant Bloom is now plunging into everything from cheap Continental holidays to aerosol air purifiers and disinfectants. All are promoted with typical Bloom abandon—in two- and three-for-one package offers and in conjunction with England's hottest new promotional tool: trading stamps . . .

'So there in London's Regent Street from his pale-lemon-carpeted headquarters last week, the restless, fast-talking Bloom cheerfully explained that he was only beginning. "I'm an idea man," he said rifling through advertising layouts on his glass-topped antique desk. "I sling my ideas out to the staff and say make them work. I look for things where the trading systems are fuddy-duddy, archaic—then I move in. Home-movie equipment—we're going to start in April. It'll be easy. The TV rental business—more than 50% of TV sets in Britain are rented. There shouldn't be any problem making money here. And think of the business when colour comes in!".'

This was written in March 1964 just about 14 weeks before the final collapse. The home movie idea was still-born; the projectors proved to be faulty. In April 1964, with sales slowing, it was decided to produce a Tallent 'rival' to Rolls which could be marketed with lower advertising costs, lower hire purchase deposits and no special offers. The 'Tallent twin' came out at the end of April at 36 guineas and 56 guineas as opposed to the 39 guineas and 59 guineas of the Concord, but it flopped from the start.

Cash was now running out fast. On 14 May the year's results were announced and although a final dividend of 120% was declared, making a total of 200%, as forecast, profits were disappointing. The net profit, after various provisions for tax showed an increase of only £11,873 over 1962 at £475,799. Rolls shares lost a further 4s 6d.

Undoubtedly, apart from any lack of confidence in Rolls machines and their selling methods, the automatic was making inroads into the market at this time and it was unfortunate that the Rolls's model had been dragging its heels. The Continent was scoured for a suitable machine and the Rolls Robot was announced in June. This was a machine bought in from Imperial Domestic Appliances, who in turn were importing from Italy. The profit margin was far too low but by the time of the launch the end of Rolls was only a few weeks away. During the whole of May only 6,504 washing machines were sold as against 7,442 in a single week of October the year before; each machine was costing nearly £22 in advertising alone.

In those last desperate weeks two final flings were announced: The Rolls Privileged Member Scheme which enabled anyone who bought a washing machine from the company to buy many other goods at far below the shop prices; and the Recommenda Rolls Scheme which rewarded people for filling in a coupon introducing a friend who bought a washing machine. Premiums offered included a watch, children's clothes or a hair drier for a single successful introduction.

Bloom started to cut his costs drastically. The Bournemouth, Swansea, Birmingham offices and depots were closed and about 80 men were trimmed from the sales force. Bloom and his co-directors took salary cuts. In a prodigious effort Rolls managed to save around £10,000 a week on their £32,000 overheads. The company still desperately needed more cash.

Stocks were sold off and £160,000 and £200,000 was

borrowed from General Guarantee, £440,000 from Capital and £200,000 from English and Overseas.

The creditors were pushing hard and the bank was considerably concerned about the overdraft. An appeal was made to Kleinworts to ask them to jointly guarantee the overdraft with Sir Isaac Wolfson. But this came to nothing. Claude Miller, a 'company doctor' was called in and agreed to investigate Rolls for a fee of £25,000, payable in advance.

Reader Harris's report to the shareholders was presented on 10 June. Profits to date for the year were substantially down and he refused to make a forecast for the year. New ventures and a 'temporary' build-up of stocks were straining the ready cash situation and it was a clear warning that more permanent finance would be needed. Rolls shares fell yet again to 13s 4½d, and English and Overseas to 16s 1½d.

On 19 June Rolls announced that they were winding up Bylock and invited Barclays Bank to appoint a receiver. At the same time Tallent, who had already laid off 50 of their 580 workers at the end of May put most of their production staff on short time. Claude Miller arrived on 23 June and, with the help of Sir Isaac Wolfson, persuaded the bank to continue Rolls's over-the-limit overdraft until the end of August. Miller was of the opinion that £1 million would see Rolls through and set about trying to raise this money. It did not prove easy. Meanwhile Rolls shares fell again to around 10s and English and Overseas took a tremendous beating.

Bloom went off to Bulgaria on 10 July in connection with his travel interests. By the time he got back 10 days later everything was over. Claude Miller, having completed his investigations, advised that unless Rolls went into liquidation the directors would become personally responsible for the company's debts.

Within a few days Edward Heath, who was at that time President of the Board of Trade, anounced that an enquiry would be held into the affairs of Rolls Razor. This enquiry and its sequel continued for nearly six years. Almost immediately Bloom was asked to resign from the chairmanship

THE COST OF PRICE-CUTTING

of English and Overseas and later he sold his shares in this company.

Towards the end of July Sir Charles Colston and Aaron Wright resigned their directorships of Rolls leaving Bloom, Al Palmer, the hire purchase director, the Jacobs brothers and Leslie Goldbart. Tallent were not slow to put in a claim for over £850,000 damages for washing machines which they said Rolls had contracted to buy over the next few years.

The Board of Trade enquiry started and dragged over a year; there were 54 days of formal hearings and 53 witnesses. There proved to be around 1,200 creditors. Barclays Bank was in for £455,381 and Pressed Steel for £434,219, a part of which was, however, disputed. After these the biggest casualties were the advertising people, of which at least one was later forced into liquidation. The total estimated Rolls deficiency was over £4 million. The liquidator stated that the company had failed basically because it was under capitalised and criticised the accounts department for failing to provide up-to-date information. At the creditors meeting Rolls shares were going at a penny a time—if anyone could be found to buy them.

Following the Board of Trade enquiry a report was sent to the Director of Public Prosecutions and the police launched their own investigation, which took a further two years. At the beginning of 1968 Bloom was arrested on two charges arising from the Board of Trade report. Sowley, the Company Secretary, Reader Harris, Al Palmer, Herbert Collins and Malcolm Cass were also implicated. Bloom had to face two indictments. The first one accused Sowley and Bloom of defrauding Rolls by falsely pretending that Electromatic's assets at 31 December 1961 were in excess of £100,000, of omittting a purchase tax liability and contingent liability in December 1961; of putting out a circular with intent to deceive Rolls shareholders which omitted to mention any such purchase tax liability and contingent liability; and of making or agreeing a false entry in a minute book.

The second indictment alleged that, with intent to deceive

K

the shareholders, Bloom made or concurred in making a statement of accounts—the Rolls balance sheet for 1963—which was false in certain respects. It also said that he made statements in a circular dated 17 September 1963 which were misleading, false or deceptive in order to persuade people to buy shares in Bylock.

Like all his co-defendants Bloom pleaded not guilty and the commital hearing went on for 115 days, making it the longest in the history of British justice. The case against Al Palmer was dismissed and he was later awarded costs in the High Court. Bloom pleaded guilty to two charges, concerning the Bylock circular and the 1963 accounts. He was eventually found guilty on these counts and was fined £20,000 in relation to the 1963 accounts and £10,000 for the Bylock circular.

In March 1970 his brother-in-law, Herbert was fined £5,000 for concurring in a false balance sheet with intent to deceive shareholders and, on the same charge and at the same time, Arthur Sowley was fined £500. Later in the year the trial of Reader Harris and Bloom's other brother-in-law Malcolm Cass came up. Reader Harris was found not guilty of concurring in making a statement in the company balance sheets with intent to deceive shareholders and which he knew to be false. A week later Malcolm Cass was acquitted of two charges against him relating to the 1963 balance sheet and the Bylock circular.

Now the dust has settled it might be worth recalling the words of Bloom's counsel, addressed to Judge Gillis: 'It would be my unhappy task to relate to your Lordship in a little detail the way in which one expert accountant after another, one adviser after another, by what can only be described as monumental neglect, prevented the building of safe financial foundations for the Rolls empire and Bloom's own fortune.' And he went on to suggest that in 1964 Bloom was a victim of a 'morass of incompetence'. This was a hapless situation for a man who was a spectacular promoter but completely un-tutored as a financier.

An Insurance Debacle

Fire, Auto and Marine
1963-1966

ELSEWHERE IN this book is recorded the sad crash of the City of Glasgow Bank nearly 100 years ago. In the British banking world a crash like this couldn't happen these days: both investors and depositors are adequately protected.

Not so in insurance. The policyholder can lose his cover overnight and this has happened to hundreds of thousands in the last decade, with some very nasty side effects especially in the motor business. In spite of some tightening up recently the law has been proved ineffective in protecting the public's interests.

One of the most disastrous and dramatic failures was that of Fire, Auto and Marine which crashed in 1966 and was headed by Dr Emil Savundra, 'affable gay host, staunch British patriot, millionaire power boat enthusiast'.

When Savundra started anyone who could produce (even, in practice, temporarily) £50,000 could begin issuing motor insurance policies and become an authorised insurer under the terms of the Road Traffic Act. And this is just what Savundra did. The Fire, Auto and Marine Insurance Company was registered on 14 February 1963, complying with the £50,000 regulation. So far so good, but it later emerged that Savundra's qualifications as an insurance man, which might reasonably be supposed to include integrity were, to say the least a little wanting.

Emil Savundra (or to give him his full name Savundra-nayagan) was born in 1923 of a well-to-do family in Colombo, Ceylon.

The first time he is known to have become involved in court proceedings was when he arranged a spectacular business deal with Communist China. Savundra at that time controlled a company known as Eastern Traders of Colombo and they undertook to supply lubricants to China through a firm called Hwa Shih. To finance the transaction Hwa Shih opened a credit amounting to 1,200,000 American dollars with a Swiss bank.

Savundra negotiated with a French company to supply the lubricants and shortly afterwards he presented the necessary documents to the Union Bank of Switzerland to obtain the payment then apparently due to him. Savundra got the money but the documents produced to the bank were subsequently found to be forgeries.

Nevertheless he returned to Ceylon $235,000 richer and declared his notes to Customs. In January 1951 Eastern Traders declared dividends at 30,000 roupees for a 10 roupee share but the Ceylon Income Tax Board assessed Savundra's tax for the year 1950 at over one million roupees. Savundra left town rather hastily and the Board seized his assets, including his car.

A few years later he was involved in what has been described as 'the case of the phantom shipment'. It was a question of phantom money because by the time this affair was over, £238,000 in gold and Swiss francs had vanished somewhere.

On 16 April 1954 the Antwerp Kredietbank received a letter from the Banco Nacional Ultramarino of Lisbon, requesting that a credit amounting to $865,000 should be opened on behalf of the Portuguese Government of Goa. The money, said the authority, should be credited to a Belgian shipping firm known as Hantra and would be used to finance the shipment of 8,000 tons of rice from Goa to a place called 'Mormugao', which was supposed to be in Portuguese Timor. A few days after this letter was received Hantra's branch office in Basle wrote saying that all the money except £5,000 should be paid to an account at the Banca Report in Lugano.

In May 1954 Graf von Honung, head of Hantra's Basle office arrived at the Antwerp bank with documents apparently certifying that the rice had been bought and loaded. Another document was presented later which stated that it had left for Mormugao aboard a Norwegian ship.

To all intents and purposes the transaction was complete and the bank transferred the money to Lugano. There somebody promptly drew £131,000 in Swiss francs and had the remaining £107,000 transferred to a Zurich bank.

The Antwerp bank then discovered, to its dismay, that the Norwegian ship was not carrying the rice at all and that the port of 'Mormugao' was apparently fictitious.

In the end four men were brought for trial in Antwerp including Savundra, who was extradited from England for the purpose. Hornung shot himself during the investigation, explaining that he had been tricked by Savundra into taking part in what he thought was a normal currency-smuggling exercise. Savundra in court hotly denied the prosecution case that he was the brains behind the fraud. He swore he had acted in good faith and the guilty party was the Goanese government which had failed to produce the rice. Savundra was sentenced to five years in prison and a 40,000 franc fine but the heart trouble with which he had suffered intermittently throughout his life in times of crisis came to his rescue and in fact he served only about 15 months, most of which time he spent in hospital.

The *Sunday Times*, using their insight team, uncovered this story without too much difficulty following Savundra's arrest. It also appears that a number of well informed people knew that he had been brought to trial in Belgium when he began Fire, Auto and Marine but the Belgian authorities were perhaps rather less than co-operative. The *Sunday Times* have stated that some time after his trial a Belgian newspaper apparently published his obituary and the police, assuming Savundra to be dead, removed his file from the public record.

In 1958 Savundra was in Accra and lived lavishly, with his wife and five children, at the Ambassador Hotel. The *Ghana Times* said he had arrived to save their country and that he was provided with £350 million (from what source it was not clear) to develop Ghana and abolish poverty once and for all.

In fact he was at that time a director of a British mining group called Camp Bird which was seeking exclusive mineral rights in Ghana. The £350 million story came from the fact that within a few weeks of his arrival he had set up four companies who together had this amount of nominal capital.

In December 1958 Camp Bird announced that it had secured the exclusive mineral rights but the Ghana government promptly denied this and the London Stock Exchange suspended dealing in Camp Bird. A couple of days later Nkrumah had Savundra deported.

Savundra turned up in London in 1962 and began trading as Fire, Auto and Marine early in 1963, doing business from a three-room office off Baker Street. As his advertising started to go out he was quickly inundated with business. That is hardly surprising since the company's motor premiums averaged half of any of the established companies and a commission of 20% attracted hundreds of insurance brokers.

In the first year Fire, Auto and Marine wrote more new motor business than any other British company and could claim a premium income of £3½ million. In the circumstances Baker Street was soon too small. First the company moved to Orchard House in Oxford Street and then to a specially built headquarters building on the North Circular Road.

Of course Savundra's meteoric rise, the amount of business he was underwriting and the rates at which he was offering cover, roused consternation in the insurance world—consternation partly because of lost business but also because it seemed certain Fire, Auto and Marine must run into trouble. The British Insurance Association appealed to the Board of Trade, who were not only worried about the possibility of a crash but also that as an insurance company Fire, Auto and Marine had legitimate ways of moving money out of the country.

Under the powers granted to them by the Insurance Companies Act 1958 the Board of Trade could demand a company's books—but only if there was a *prima-facie* case of insolvency. In spite of the representations from BIA the Board of Trade thought they could not do this. They argued that they did not have sufficient evidence. So, just a week before Fire, Auto and Marine applied to go into liquidation, a Board of Trade spokesman said, 'On the evidence available, there appears to be no immediate danger of insolvency.'

For a time it seemed as though the critics were wrong. Savundra lived like a lord and spent prodigious sums on lavish entertaining and his great love, power boat racing. He even founded Sea Unicorn Engineering Ltd to build supercharged marine engines for his boats and he owned two Aston Martins, a Rolls and a Jaguar. Not content with the success in motor insurance he went into fields that the established companies would not look at, such as insuring cigarette smokers against lung cancer. During 1964 he also spent a great deal of money funding a number of small and rather insolvent companies, most of them situated in the West Country.

For the first 18 months Fire, Auto and Marine had plenty of cash to spare. Premiums were coming in at around £50,000 a week and in those early days claims were relatively light.

However, in the autumn and early winter of 1965 claims began to catch up with income just as the insurance pundits said they would. But Savundra remained calm, explaining that the company was having teething troubles but that their flexibility, money-saving efficiency in dealing with proposals, and their 'low overheads' would speedily right the position. In any case the accounts showed that part of the income from premiums had been put into investments amounting to over £850,000 in Burmah Oil, GUS, Simon Engineering, Distillers and Beaverbrook Newspapers.

In April 1966 it became obvious that these reserves should

now be committed and Savundra's co-directors put him under some considerable pressure on this score. The auditors, also, were anxious to see these valuable share certificates forming the reserve assets and they approached Stuart de Quincey Walker, an old personal friend of Savundra's and managing director of Fire, Auto and Marine for reassurance. The auditors were stalled because it was explained that there was a delay in geting the certificates over from Zurich where they were kept by a company known as Merchants and Finance Trust which had provided Fire, Auto and Marine with its original capital.

However the certificates finally arrived later in April 1966 and the auditors took down the details before returning them to Zurich. All right, said Savundra's co-directors, the auditors are satisfied but surely now is the time to sell some of these shares to bolster the company's position?

Savundra was, however, curiously reluctant and instead proposed that he should go to America and raise some fresh money. On 10 May 1966 he left for America returning three weeks later unsuccessful.

Savundra now began to negotiate the sale of the company and, not unexpectedly, those he approached asked to see the accounts. It did not take them very long to enquire about the interest on the shares invested which should have been in the region of £100,000. Apparently Savundra had no reply to this and huffily broke off negotiations.

In June Savundra resigned from the Board—his heart was playing up again—and he transferred his controlling interest in Fire, Auto and Marine to de Quincey Walker. It was reported at the time that he did this for a mere £4,000. The Board, now thoroughly alarmed, asked the auditors, Fisher, Conway, Fenton & Company for details of the investment schedule which they had been shown.

Savundra now decided to go to a Swiss clinic for the sake of his health and the directors sent Walker to Zurich to realise the shares. He returned on 28 June 1966 with a letter from Merchants and Finance Trust's attorney (Dr Paul Hagenbach) explaining that the funds were deposited with Merchants and Finance Trust on a 10 year fixed interest loan at 4%.

This of course was the end of the company. In insurance reserve assets must be liquid and they must be realisable promptly. Hagenbach was prepared to produce the share certificates but they would only be sent to London on condition that they were returned immediately and they were to remain the property of Merchants and Finance Trust although Fire, Auto and Marine would be shown as owners on the certificates.

A day later the board heard further bad news. It appeared that the share certificates were not genuine.

Immediately following the collapse the *Sunday Times* conducted a masterly survey of the machinations of the Savundra empire and provided the companies concerned with the serial numbers of the certificates as noted by the auditors. The chairman of Burmah Oil (a holding of £226,000) immediately said they 'must be fraudulent'. GUS, in which Fire, Auto and Marine were supposed to hold £213,750 of shares at the then current valuation stated that the dates or numbers must be wrong or they were fraudulent. The other three companies replied in precisely the same terms. By now, very seriously alarmed, the company chairman, Cecil Tross-Youle called an emergency meeting and asked for an independent report from Cork Gully, the City accountants, who, on 4 July, reported there were 'certain irregularities in the investment portfolio'. The Board of Fire, Auto and Marine, minus Savundra, decided to apply for a compulsory winding up order and Tross-Youle personally delivered the petition to the Law Courts. Meanwhile his co-directors Cecil Jager and Joseph Gordon went to Scotland Yard to make a report to the fraud squad of what they had discovered. In the enquiry that followed it quickly became apparent that Tross-Youle, Jager and Gordon had been taken for a ride. And it speedily emerged, too, that somewhere along the line over £1 million of Fire, Auto and Marine's assets had been salted away. Even Savundra, the luxury liver, could not have spent all this personally: he must have established a cache somewhere.

In the autumn of 1966 the Official Receiver estimated the company's debts at £2,310,000 with a deficiency in the region of £1,410,000.

The Board of Trade investigation had begun earlier in the year in the absence of both the principal directors, Emil Savundra and Stuart de Quincey Walker. Savundra was at that time still in Ceylon and in December it was reported that de Quincey Walker had sold his Hampton Court home and gone abroad. Savundra had now been overseas for five months following a claimed coronary thrombosis, for which he was treated in Zurich. From the clinic he issued a statement denying all responsibility for the company's collapse and stating that he had sold it to Walker on 21 June when it was in a healthy financial state.

Meanwhile the Official Receiver lodged papers with the Director of Public Prosecutions to consider whether any proceedings were called for. And no less than 230,000 motorists slowly recovered from the shock of finding themselves with completely worthless policies.

Savundra did in fact make a reappearance in London, on 15 January. He said at the time: 'I have returned because I have sufficient faith in British justice and because I intend to prosecute libel actions against certain scurrilous rags.' By now it was becoming clear that not only were the share certificates fakes but that at least £450,000 of policyholders' money had been systematically funnelled out of Britain.

At the beginning of February 1967 Savundra, now 'co-operating' with the Board of Trade, was foolish enough to risk a television confrontation with David Frost.

Frost set the scene well, briefly going over Savundra's earlier business scandals and then explaining how Fire, Auto and Marine had built up a premium income of over £5 million in less than two years. Frost indicated that Fire, Auto and Marine had failed because both Savundra and Walker had had their hands in the till. He said that the Liechtenstein Bank, Merchants Finance Trust, was in fact controlled by the two directors and that nearly £1 million of Fire, Auto and Marine funds had been deposited with Merchants Finance Trust which in turn had loaned £380,000 to Savundra and £200,00 to Walker as individuals. Under the agreements which they concluded with themselves, wearing their different hats, the loans could not be recovered for 20 years.

Savundra faced an angry audience which Frost could not always control. He was challenged by two women who had both lost a husband in a car crash and then failed to get any insurance money. Savundra suggested that justice had been done because the Fire, Auto and Marine policy contained a clause which excluded liability if a car in an accident 'was being driven in an unsafe or unroadworthy condition or manner'. A Lloyds underwriter commented afterwards: 'This rules out everything but an Act of God,'—and is a salutary reminder to read the small print in *everything*. Frost nearly had a riot on his hands when Savundra suggested that by selling out he had no legal or moral responsibility.

Frost closed the interview thus:

'Let me just say one last question. You can look at these people here . . . widows, widowers, whoever they are and you can feel "I have no legal responsibility"?'

'Right,' said Savundra.

' "And I've signed a piece of paper and I have no moral responsibility either?" '

To which Savundra replied again, 'Right'.

But nemesis was near at hand. On 11 February 1967 Savundra and Walker appeared in court at Ealing and both were remanded in custody, bail being refused, despite an impassioned plea from Savundra's counsel, Mr Ian McCulloch, who claimed: 'It is monstrous that there should have been a trial by television and trial by the *Sunday Times*.' At the same time McCulloch told the court that an application would be made soon to commit the *Sunday Times* and 'a certain other person' for contempt. In fact nothing came of this application and one of the remarkable sidelights on the whole sorry Fire, Auto and Marine business is the part which this famous national newspaper played in so speedily and efficiently completing a preliminary investigation long before any official bodies had made any significant moves. No doubt it was all very good copy but the fact remains that the investigations of the *Sunday Times* provided the Board of Trade with a great deal of information at an early date and the newspaper made available to the investigators a number of key documents which they had obtained.

At the preliminary hearing Savundra was charged that in July 1965 'with intent to defraud, he uttered a forged security purporting to be a certificate evidencing the holding of 3% Savings Bonds, value £510,500.15.10d; between July 1 and September 4 with intent to defraud he was concerned in making a false entry in a balance sheet forming part of the accounts of Fire, Auto and Marine Insurance Company, purporting to show that on April 30 1965, the company held British Securities valued at £540,000.' Stuart de Quincey Walker was arraigned on the same charges.

Savundra and de Quincey Walker were finally brought to trial on a total of six charges each including conspiracy to defraud, uttering false documents and conspiring to make false entries on balance sheets. Savundra was found guilty on five counts and Walker on four. On 7 March 1968 Savundra was sentenced to eight years plus a fine of £50,000 and an order to pay costs; Walker was sentenced to five years and to pay costs. Both men were banned from holding directorships of British companies for five years after their release from prison.

Apart from the astonishing part played by the press in revealing Savundra's swindles, the whole episode made it painfully clear that the British public were almost wholly unprotected when buying insurance. Of course, the purchaser *should* read the small print; of course he *should* be cautious about cut rates, but 230,000 weren't in the case of Fire, Auto and Marine alone. Not only did some of these suffer very heavily for their gullibility but many others, too, who perhaps had never heard of Fire, Auto and Marine until they tried to claim on one of its policyholders.

Index